The Age of the Female: A Thousand Years of Yin

The Age of the Female

A Thousand Years of Yin

by

Richard Andrew King

Richard King Publications

© by Richard Andrew King
Published by Richard King Publications
PO Box 3621
Laguna Hills, CA 92654

Library of Congress Cataloging-in-Publication Data

King, Richard Andrew
The Age of the Female: A Thousand Years of Yin
ISBN: 978-0-931872-03-7
Publication date: 5 March 2008

DEDICATION

To Christa and Chandra, my beloved daughters,
whose hearts, minds and spirits are the
epitome of what it is to be female,
and whose inherent beauty in all they do
inspired this work.

ACKNOWLEDGMENTS

Many thanks to Chris Grau for his technical expertise.

My extended appreciation to Kaye Young for her
endless support and belief in this work.

Thanks also to Shannon Yarbrough,
author of Stealing Wishes, for his
cover design assistance.

Richard Andrew King
PO Box 3621
Laguna Hills, CA 92654-3621
www.richardking.net

THE AGE OF THE FEMALE
A Thousand Years of Yin

Table of Contents

King

The Age of the Female: A Thousand Years of Yin

INTRODUCTION

The rise of the female has been an extraordinary event in world history. In what is basically a blink of cosmic time, she has sprung upon the great life stage with an outstanding entrance. Females now occupy positions and places of prestige reserved exclusively to her male counterpart just a few decades ago. Within the dawning of this modern world, women have become presidents and prime ministers of nations, cabinet members of world governments, admirals and generals of military forces, captains of manned space flights, billionaire entrepreneurs, titans of industry, leaders of corporations, doctors, lawyers, police officers, fire fighters, presidents of educational institutions and a whole host of other prestigious titles. Such a rapid rise in prominence begs the question, "Why?"

In this cause and effect universe nothing is happenstance. There is order to everything, even though we may not initially understand it. Within that order there are answers. We just have to dig deeply into the universal fabric of the "not as yet known" to find them. This book is the result of digging into that fabric using the science of numerology, of searching for answers to the relatively rapid ascent of the female in our world. As I searched for answers, I kept finding answers, incredible answers, answers so overwhelming to me as a professional numerologist I felt compelled to share them. Symbols and numbers are two of the languages God uses

King

to communicate with man. The dawning of female prominence on our earth is profoundly depicted in both symbols and numbers of people, places, objects and events of the 19th and 20th Centuries. The information offered here is for your consideration, and to me it is overwhelming proof that, indeed, the Age of the Female has arrived and it is now her time to take center stage on the great stage of earth.

Richard Andrew King

CHAPTER ONE

A THOUSAND YEARS OF YIN

A thousand years of Yang, gone.
A thousand years of him, been.
Now, a thousand years of Yin begin
as the cosmic clock assures
and the tides of time secure –
the next one thousand years
belong to her.

December 31st 1999, marked the last day of the last month of the last thousand years, a millennium in which the male energy, the Yang, the One (1), dominated. But that time has passed. It is no more. Feminine rays are now being cast by the cosmic sun and it is time for the female energy, the Yin, the Two (2) to take her place on the great life stage. Irrefutably, with the dawning of the year 2000, the Age of the Female has arrived.

King

NUMBERS

"Numbers rule the universe. Everything is arranged according to number and mathematical shape." This profound statement was made by the famous mathematician/scientist, Pythagoras, approximately twenty-five hundred years ago. It is this fact which corroborates the rise of the female – a prodigious event in world history whose occurrence has clearly not been accidental.

Numbers rule the universe because everything can be reduced to numbers. And what are numbers? They are nothing more than symbols, ciphers and codes depicting, illustrating, defining and describing life and its functions. Do away with numbers and civilization as we know it would collapse. Light, sound, music, computers, financial institutions, commercial enterprise, scientific research and media communication would all be non-existent. Life, as we know it, would come to a screeching halt were it not for numbers. Incontrovertibly, life is numbers, and when we think about it there is nothing that does not have a numerical foundation, including millennia.

Besides being a renowned mathematician, scientist and philosopher of his time, Pythagoras was also regarded as being the first numerologist – one who associates numbers with life. Even the famous Greek philosopher, Aristotle, wrote: "The Pythagorean . . . having been brought up in the study of mathematics, thought that things are numbers . . . and that the whole cosmos is a scale and a number." (qtd. in O'Connor and Robertson). Thus, because of Pythagoras, numerology – the art and science of numbers and their relationship to life – was born.

Numerology has merit. It is a science as well as an art, just like medicine. It may not maintain a sense of public acceptance or awareness at this time, but that does not invalidate its reality. There was a time, as we are all aware, when the consensus of the earth's population believed the earth was flat and that the four corners of the world were, indeed, four corners. Then Columbus came along and altered the consensus of the public consciousness. The world was now round, not flat, and those believing differently were simply living in the past, and any knowledge such believers espoused about the earth being flat were simply erroneous.

Numerology, a mathematical tool for understanding the framework of life, is simply one of those bodies of knowledge lying underneath the surface of the vast ocean of visible form. As a metaphysical science, numerology will gain acceptance during this next millennium as its truth is revealed. The positive thing about numerology is that it can be proven; its truth determined scientifically, and the scientific truth is that the next thousand years will be ruled by all things Yin.

Furthermore, it's an acknowledged fact that simply because something is not openly active and generally obvious it does not necessarily lack merit. Science is the discipline of discovering the unknown, of making the imperceptible, perceptible. In the last thousand years, science concentrated on external realities. With the turning of the millennia tide, more attention will now be given to internal realities. Being the solo player, for example, a function of male One (1) energy will, in part, be openly replaced by partnership and teamwork, a feminine Two (2) trait.

There will be other visible changes. Men will soften, become more receptive, sensitive, caring, intuitive. In fact, science is now proving that intuition is a reality and that many top executives use their intuitive skills to solve problems. This trend will definitely increase and the best of the best will be sought, not just for their logic, but for their gut instincts as well. Is this to say that all men will become feminine during this new age? Of course not. But the paradigm of what a man and woman were during the last thousand years is definitely undergoing a metamorphosis, as any sentient soul will acknowledge.

Numerology is neither back room hocus-pocus nor crystal ball gazing. It is science – an empirical method of ascertaining the super-structure and divine design of life. It is no less real than the genetic code or the atomic structure of elements. It has existed since time immemorial, and the world should be forever grateful to Pythagoras for his enlightened genius which opened the door to the inner reality and secrets of life through numbers.

CHANCE OR DESIGN

Is it by chance that the next thousand years will be the Age of the Female and embrace her energy? No. It is by design, spiritual-cosmic design. Order is the first law of the universe, and just as the great cosmic pendulum swayed within the polar field of the One (1) vibration for the last thousand years, it has now reversed its direction, passed the polar midpoint and is transiting the energy field of the Two (2).

Hermes Trismegistus, the alleged teacher of the magical system known as Hermiticism, is said to have provided the wisdom of light in the ancient mysteries of Egypt. He said that if a pendulum swings one way, it must, by its very nature, swing the other. From positive pole to negative pole and back again ceaselessly sways the great cosmic clock to a timeless, relentless rhythm, a rhythm which honored *him* for the last thousand years but which, by predictable circle, cycle and tide, will now honor *her* for the next thousand.

16

The Hour Glass of
Circles, Cycles and Sides

Life is a construct of circles, cycles and sides –
timeless tides of constantly-flowing energy
swaying to and fro to the polar rhythm
of the Great Cosmic Pendulum.
Within this flux is the crux
of man's secret identity –
his coming and going,
rising and falling,
crying, sighing,
living, dying,
laughing,
smiling,
tears, fears,
relentless years –
endless revolution.
Helpless to challenge
the forces which move him,
man's hope is to understand
the infinite Source sustaining him,
to honor, embrace and surrender to It;
to accept and adjust to the Reality of that
which is, avoiding the illusion of that which is not.

The Age of the Female: A Thousand Years of Yin

OTHER TRAITS

The gigantic millennia shift from Yang to Yin has also been responsible for earthman's debarkation from his own world in efforts to explore other worlds and celestial bodies such as our own moon, the planet mars and beyond. In fact, the moon has not only been regarded throughout the history of mankind as feminine by nature, it is also ruled by the number Two (2). Therefore, it certainly isn't a coincidence that earthman landed on the moon when he did, in the Twentieth Century - a Two (2) cipher in reduction $(20 = 2 + 0 > 2)$.

Other signposts of this age are the focus on relationships, the rise of competitive athletics, especially for females; gangs, terrorism, the advancement of IT technologies, personal data collection, invasion of privacy, sexual gender issues, teamwork and partnership, the morass of confusion accosting and besieging the general public, mostly because of these numerical polar shifts; the expansion of networking in the business world; the rise of women, not only in business, but in all walks of life, and the exposure of hidden knowledge, which will become more obvious as the millennium matures.

As an example of these changes, remember when fathers would shake their son's hands rather than give them a hug or a kiss or a supportive word of encouragement because fatherly hugs and kisses to a son were deemed inappropriate? Remember when it was

King

unmanly for a man to cry in public or express any 'feminine' emotion, even in the isolation of his own privacy? No? Well, there was a time when fathers in general would only shake their son's hands and never show them physical affection. There was a time when men would not cry in public because to do so was thought to be a violation of their masculinity. There was a time when the only support a child got from his father was silence and indifference because such behaviors were thought to make young men strong. It was the mother who was the primary nurturer, not the father. That model is now changing.

Interestingly, parenting and spousal roles are clearly undergoing a metamorphosis. The former image of the male being the bread-winner is changing, as well as the mother being the primary nurturer. It is not unusual to have the female part of the household now earning more than her male counterpart, and fathers are taking a much more active role in the raising of their children. It is not uncommon in divorce cases to have primary custody of the children being awarded to the father, not the mother. Too, since women have entered the workplace, many of the physical ailments normally associated with men are on the rise in women. Whereas in the not too distant past only one income was sufficient to manage the affairs of a household, now it generally requires two.

All of these characteristics are attributable to the gigantic vibrational wave of Two (2) energy which has now, like the tidal wave of a completely new ocean, washed over us, encircling, entangling, embroiling, embracing, engaging, enveloping, enlightening, involving, saturating and surrounding us with, and even submerging us in, its aqueous presence. Without a doubt, during the next thousand years feminine energy will rain upon the earth and the female, having been subordinate for the last thousand years, will now reign supreme.

THE CLASH OF OPPOSITES

The change of millennia from One to Two energy is not to be taken lightly. One and Two are exact opposites in form and function. Therefore, the enormous shift from one set of energy characteristics to the other can cause, and often does, extreme havoc.

As we know, men and women have a difficult time understanding one another because they're opposites. Each gender processes information differently from the other and is motivated by contrasting desires. While men tend to be logical, insensitive, direct, active and unbending, women tend to be emotional, intuitive, indirect, passive and adaptable. Men hunt, women support. Men like looking; women like being looked at. These are not casual differences. They are intrinsically diametrically opposed gender-rooted issues, and their differences have created challenges and problems between the sexes since the beginning of time.

The last thousand years was primarily electrified and energized with masculine matter and substance. However, that has now been replaced with female vibratory matter and substance. Our world now exists in a millennium mist of energies exactly opposite from the last thousand years. See the problem? And because the shift is still new, the earth is still in its adjustment/gestation phase and will be until approximately the year Twenty-One Hundred (2100). Whether the phrase "it's a man's world" will be adjusted to "it's a woman's world" remains to be seen, but the reality of the matter is, it is a whole new world we're living in, a world dominated by feminine, not masculine, energy. Those who can adjust will survive; those who can't are in for a more-than-bumpy ride.

Caution, however, should be offered to those people who jump too high and too far for joy at the receipt of such news. As everything in this creation has two sides, one positive and one negative, so does the Two (2) vibration. Female characteristics, as those of the male, have positive and negative tendencies. Look at the last thousand years of male-dominated energy. There were good and bad aspects to it. So it is with this new thousand year cycle. There will be good times. There will be bad times. There will be ups. There will be downs. There will be bask-in-the-sun periods of beautiful weather and there will be tumultuous storms. It's the nature of life.

The Age of the Female: A Thousand Years of Yin

Here's another caution – one for gender enthusiasts. In consideration of the grand circle and cycle of life in which what goes around comes around, the possibility exists of a person being one gender in one life and the opposite gender in a subsequent life. An over-exuberant female, for example, might one day be reincarnated as a man in a woman's world, or an over-exuberant male could be incarnated as a female in another life. This would tend to bring into stasis a consciousness in disequilibrium. Nature always works to balance, and getting too far to the edge of the male or female polarity will always bring a reconciliation and adjustment of the energies involved. Bodies are just shells encasing the soul. Gender can change from life to life. Therefore, we should appreciate our gender but not cling to it for, in reality, the soul has no gender.

For those who do not believe in or subscribe to the possibility of reincarnation, the thought is offered that energy can neither be created nor destroyed. Since our souls are divine energy, they cannot be destroyed and, therefore, are constantly taking on a new form when the current one wears out or is discarded in some way. There is no universal spiritual law which says that once a man, always a man or once a woman, always a woman. Genders change. How poetically just it would be for any of us to take on the opposite form in another life from the one to which we were, perhaps, overtly attached to in this life.

King

Let it also be known that the female energy taking precedence during this millennium is not restricted to form or gender alone. *The feminine Two (2) energy affects and pervades every living thing on this planet regardless of gender.* Therefore, the Age of the Female is not so much about form as it is about energy. In other words, everyone will also be infused with the cosmic currents of the female vibration, even more than they have been in the past. Every one of us is a mixture of masculine and feminine energy, not to be equated with 'macho' and 'effeminate'. There is, for example, no numerology chart totally devoid of either One or Two energy. We all have these vibrations in our basic composition. Masculine and feminine are simply two of the contrasting words used to describe the intrinsic polarities found in nature.

OTHER APPELLATIONS

This Age of the Female could have other appellations. The number Two also rules 'other people' and, therefore, this millennium might also be known as the *Age of Others*. Additional labels could be the *Age of Relationship*, the *Age of Teamwork*, the *Age of Conflict and Resolution*, the *Age of Diplomacy* – all concepts falling under the rulership of the Two energy.

This 2nd Millennium is also the *Age of Duality*, so anything having to do with opposing polarities will be intensified and brought into focus in a major way. Thus,

The Age of the Female: A Thousand Years of Yin

our inevitable battle and struggle with good versus evil will not only continue to course through our veins, it will ooze from our pores, saturating our lives with moral, ethical and spiritual choices unlike any with which we have had to contend heretofore.

The positive solution – always make the "Up Choice," that choice which takes us upward, not downward; that choice which moves us in the direction of that which is pure and noble rather than that which is impure and ignoble; that choice which directs us into the comforting and edifying illumination of the Light, as opposed to that which leads us down the ladder of life into the abysmal morass of cold, dark, dank and dismal labyrinthine dungeons where shadows are non-existent – a scary thought because shadows cannot exist without even a scintilla of light.

If there is any one challenge besetting the Age of the Female, it will be balance – the act of bringing equilibrium to opposing forces, ideals, philosophies, egos. Our world is now too small, too compact, too full of global issues affecting everyone for everyone not to be concerned about each other. It is really a time to learn to get along, to embrace tolerance, understanding, patience and kindness. We're all in this boat called 'Earth' together, and if we rock it back and forth too drastically without concern for its seaworthy stability, we run the risk of sinking it, more now than ever before.

King

Even on a personal level, our individual goal should be to always work to balance, even if the world seems to be running wild and teeter-tottering dangerously out of control. In fact, under this 11/2 vibration there is the distinct possibility of intranational as well as international global rivalries. Terrorism, for example, is now a fact of everyday life on a world basis, just as street gangs are a fact of daily life in major cities throughout many countries. Individually, we may not be able to balance the macroscopic world, but we can balance our own personal microscopic worlds, and just because the world may be out of balance does not mean we have to be. In fact, maintaining a personal state of stasis may well be our best defense from being embroiled in any external confusion and chaos which might arise from the discord of conflicting, opposing polarities during this age.

SUMMARY

All in all, the Age of the Female, this thousand years of Yin, will be an exciting and dynamic time for the inhabitants of earth because our consciousness as a one-world people will be undergoing an extreme metamorphosis, especially in the first one hundred years. This is not an age which will focus on that which is singular, separate or autonomous. This is an age which is and will continue to be involved with those energies which are relationship and partnership oriented; on that which is equal, fair and balanced; on that which is saturated with others being involved with others. It is the time for females and feminine energy to have their due, a time where emotion and intuition will wax like the fullness of the moon on a clear and starry night. Thus, there will be reflection as well as creation; absorption as well as radiation. There will be opposition and contrast, confliction and distinction. This new age will be an age which will rock, teeter-totter, swing and sway to energies far more powerful than man's ability to control or manipulate. It is an age in which we would be well-served to buckle up, hang on, stay balanced, disciplined, kind and caring because, to be sure, we're in for the ride of our lives.

The Age of the Female: A Thousand Years of Yin

CHAPTER TWO

MILLENNIA SHIFT

Tick, tock, swing, sway;
back and forth, night and day;
up and down, ever round,
circles, cycles, sides abound.
Tectonic rifts, millennia shift;
Yang and Yin revolve again.
Tick-tock, tick-tock,
ever swings the cosmic clock;
ever shifting rival roles;
relentless tides;
conflicting poles.
Tick-tock, tick-tock, tick-tock.

Millennium 2000! It is definitely a hallmark for planet earth and a gigantic transition for its inhabitants. January 1st, 2000, marked an enormous change for all of us now occupying mother earth for the next thousand years, a period which will be far different from anything we have ever known heretofore.

King

With this shift in millennia from a 1 vibration to a 2, the Cosmic Pendulum has swung to its opposite polarity generating a complete *bouleversement*, a total reversal of polar energies from masculine to feminine. Indeed, the whole focus of life known to us earthlings for the last thousand years has not only changed, but it has changed to its exact opposite polarity, a totally antithetical energy field with completely contrasting characteristics.

It is this total reversal of energies which has caused a great deal of confusion for planet earth, confusion poignantly felt, especially by those born in the Twentieth Century because they still have attitudinal, emotional, psychological, social, moral and ethical remnants of the 1900s coursing through their veins, flowing through their hearts and imbedded in their heads. Their memories are of a very different time, a time never to come again.

In former times, a man's word was his bond. Now his bond is encumbered with legalese and self-serving fine print tucked away in the foreboding recesses of a contractual quagmire. In times past people could walk around their neighborhoods, safely, greeting their neighbors by name and never even giving a thought to being robbed, assaulted, raped, shot or kidnapped; when people would neither lock the doors to their homes or cars at night for fear of intrusion; when the phrase 'latchkey kid' was non-existent. It was a time when a child would never think of suing his parents, when

The Age of the Female: A Thousand Years of Yin

professional athletes played solely for the love of the game, where companies valued loyalty, wars were fought openly; where identity theft, invasion of privacy, spam, computer viruses, cell phones and instant media madness didn't exist because the degree of technology was far more limited. It was also a time, sadly, when women were not favored in the workplace, let alone receiving equal pay for equal work or being placed in positions of authority such as CEOs, presidents, generals, admirals, police officers, doctors, lawyers and titans of industry. The litany is endless.

All in all, the last thousand years was a very different time, a time of Yang, a time of the male; a time long gone. It was basically an age manifesting a clear line of debarkation between the two sexes, their roles, functions, attributes and expectations. Basically, for right or wrong, it was a time when things were generally singular, direct, clearly defined.

However, with the enormous Cyclopean shift of millennia energy, the obverse view of the cosmic coin has changed and the image on the coin is now that of woman and all things Yin. Perspectives, viewpoints, outlooks and mindscape are now, unquestionably and incontestably, female.

Interestingly, and quite notably, the face on the first U.S. coin of the Two Millennium is that of Sacagawea, the Shoshone Indian woman who played a vital role as guide, interpreter and diplomat during the historic Lewis

King

and Clark expedition of 1804 to 1806. Without her, the expedition would most likely have perished. Too, the Sacagawea dollar coin was predated by that of Susan B. Anthony, one of the women who led the suffrage movement in the Eighteen to early Nineteen Hundreds. This commemorative coin was circulated in 1979, just twenty-one years before the turn of the millennium, a cosmic eye-blink before yang yielded to yin.

Is it coincidental that Sacagawea and Susan B. Anthony are honored on the coins of American money at the precise time of the Millennia Shift? No. This is simply how the energy of the 2 has manifested itself. There are no coincidences nor accidents in the universe. It was the male who occupied (during the Yang era), and still primarily occupies, the collection of images on U. S. currency. These men obviously deserve to be where they are. Who could challenge putting George Washington, Abraham Lincoln, Benjamin Franklin, et. al. on United States currency? After all, they did exist in the millennium of the male 1 energy, and their accomplishments were prodigious to the ideal of free men everywhere.

However, with the emergence of the feminine energy, it is also fitting and proper that the female receive her acclaim for her contributions. These two examples of Sacagawea and Susan B. Anthony being celebrated on the coins of U.S. currency are simple illustrations of how the Yin energy is influencing the world. Indeed, Mother earth has now been magnetized to the matriarchal mist of the female force and there is no turning back. The time frame of this new millennium is, and will be, a cosmic celebration of Her.

SHIFTING SEASONS

There seems to be some question as to when the Second Millennium actually began. One thought is that it began in the year 2001. Actually, it began in the first second of the first day of January 2000. A simple analogy will help clarify this fact. When a child is born, we don't label him a particular age until he is one year old, at which time we say he is a year old. Factually, he has been alive for twelve months and the beginning of his life in terms of age began in the first second he exited the womb. So it was for Millennium 2000. She took her first infant breath in that first second of the year Two Thousand. In saluting her birth, may she have a peaceful, balanced, kind, caring, harmonious, happy and wholesome life.

"To everything there is a season, and a time to every purpose under the heaven." This Biblical reference (King James Version, Eccles. 3.1) underscores the reality of the circles, cycles, sides and tides of life which is not just a Christian philosophy but a universal truism echoed in every scientific and mystical teaching of the world. Everything has its season. Everything has its time. Everything has its purpose. So it is with millennia.

King

Each has its season, time and purpose, as well as its intrinsic set of characteristics. Furthermore, the shifts between millennia, especially between those vibrations which are diametrically opposed – the 1 and 2; 4 and 5; 7 and 8 – are intense and dramatic. It's like going from night to day or hot to cold. "Tumultuous" describes their transitions well.

Millennia are huge living waves of cosmic energy. They roll onto and over the beach of time with absolutely no regard for personalities, possessions or social conventions. Oblivious to their predecessor, they have their own will and they exercise it mercilessly. They are aloof, indifferent and inconsiderate of what lies in their path. These thousand year periods of impersonal, irrepressible power and time harbor gargantuan levels of energy far beyond the ability of any human being to control or manipulate. Truthfully, they control us. The sheer weight of their mass and energy compels us to move to their will and in their direction. Indeed, they move us where they choose and when they choose, for we are not strong enough to swim against them any more than we are strong enough to swim against the force of a tidal wave. In effect, they rule and we obey.

Fortunately, millennia and their intrinsic characteristics are calculable, moving to a predetermined rhythm, and by understanding their essence and adjusting to them, we can survive by surfing, by going with their flow. Resisting them is futile. Were we to do

The Age of the Female: A Thousand Years of Yin

so, they would simply pick us up, like the towering wave, and slam us down into a seabed of sand and shells, humbling us in the process.

Because of the enormity of their cosmic force and weight, changes in millennia are, likewise, enormous. Each millennium has very different traits and characteristics, just as do numbers. To remain rooted in the ways of an outgoing millennium and not adapt to the energies and characteristics of the incoming one is risky. Such is the dilemma the world is in today. It is caught in a state of transition between these colossal and dynamic periods of time – the outgoing 1 male energy of the last millennium and the incoming, diametrically oppositional 2 female energy of the current millennium. Furthermore, if it (the world) does not change, adapt and adjust to the shifting of the new energies now enveloping us, our world flirts with destruction, hardship and our own annihilation, either on a personal or global level.

YANG vs. YIN

Simply stated, opposites oppose. Their contradictory natures make them antagonistic. Such dissimilarity creates enigmatic differences, misunderstandings, apprehensions, tensions. It's like Night trying to understand Day and Day, Night or, in more practical arenas, men trying to understand women and vice versa. Even though both components of the pairs are parts of the same whole, there are challenges in understanding each other. This idea is echoed in "Ballad of East and West" by Rudyard Kipling: "Oh, East is East and West is West, and never the twain shall meet, Till Earth and Sky stand presently at God's great Judgment Seat."

East/West, North/South, day/night, man/woman, hot/cold, in/out, up/down, back/forth, on/off, hard/soft, push/pull, inhale/exhale, winners/losers – the world is a construct of opposites. It is dual in nature. Science and spirituality both concur on this point and there is no escaping its truth.

This concept of polar opposites is clearly and simply depicted in the Yin/Yang symbol of the Chinese Tao. Notice the picture below. It is familiar to all of us.

Simple, beautiful and timeless in design, this universal image is profound in its meaning. The white side is the Yang or male influence. The black side is the Yin or female influence. Within the white side is a black dot representing female energy and within the black side is a white dot representing male energy. The line between them is curved and all is contained within the same circle of completeness.

The Age of the Female: A Thousand Years of Yin

What this symbol is saying in effect is that the natural construct of life in this creation is dual in nature and that each polarity contains within its energy field the essence of the other, so neither is sovereign unto itself and each is actually interdependent upon and intertwined with the other. The differences between the polarities are not cut and dry and their mutual energies ebb and flow within the context of the whole. Nothing is either all black or all white, all positive or all negative, all masculine or all feminine, all good or all bad. Both hemispheres of the entire sphere are equal and necessary. Neither is superior. Each is a fundamental component of creation.

As has been mentioned, the last thousand years have been dominated by the '1' vibration. In numerology 'One' represents the 'yang' of the Chinese Tao, the masculine energy. 'One' is a fire sign. Its symbol is the sun. It is extremely active, direct, dynamic, assertive, aggressive, creative, initiating, rational, independent, unbending, ego driven, self-oriented, straight forward, positive, different and unique. 'One' also rules monarchs, matriarchs, patriarchs and authority figures. Ones lead and are self-starters. They go first and show the way. Ones stand alone and usually stand for something. They are strong, sometimes stubborn, courageous and unique. Ones are doers, lone wolves, mavericks, pioneers, explorers, conquerors; never followers.

These qualities and characteristics of the 1 energy have been the basis of the framework of the last millennium, that time period between the years 1000 and 1999. In reflection, this cosmic interlude was devoted to the emergence of sovereign, independent and autonomous nations emerging on the global scene, engaging in activities of conquest, the planting of flags and claiming lands for king, crown and country. It was a rough and rugged time full of exploration, pioneering, discovery, personal courage, industrialization, invention, conflict, open and direct warfare; a time saturated and over-flowing with male-dominated energy. Arguably, the first millennium was the beginning of socialization and civilization for modern man.

On the other hand, the now ubiquitous Two millennium of the Yin exists in direct contrast to its predecessor. Two, symbolized by the moon, is a water sign. In contrast to the One, positive Two traits are emotional, kind, caring, sensitive, receptive, intuitive, supportive, sharing, helping, assisting. Two is generally regarded from a numerological perspective as being the energy of interpersonal relationship; it is outwardly passive, non-assertive, dependent, diplomatic, bending, acquiescent, indirect and others-oriented. Two is the team player, the one who cooperates, collaborates, harmonizes, equalizes and negotiates. However, in consideration of the other side of its coin, Two can also be combative, competitive, argumentative, interfering, disputatious, contradictory, indecisive, deceitful, duplicitous and truculent.

During the One era the discovery phase of earth was accomplished. Nations established their territory and sovereignty. But the world has now shrunk. No longer can any country stand alone. The complexities of survival – nationally and globally – mandate a new and different mindset. Nations must now embrace the qualities of the Two – cooperation, togetherness, partnership, relationship and support. The Second Millennium will undoubtedly be a time when the focus will be on others, relationships, getting along, cooperating, supporting, serving, caring, sharing, tolerating, balancing and equalizing.

The problem, however, is that in the negative aspects of the Two (conflict, opposition, emotion, competition, imbalance, deceit, duplicity and darkness) man will be subjected to many challenges on a global level, and if he is not careful, his lack of attentiveness to the higher ideals of the Two (peace, balance, patience, caring, helping) could well be his ultimate undoing. It is up to man in general, and each individual in particular, to express the highest qualities of the Two if there is to be any kind of peace, individually or collectively. There are simply too many people and nations with disparate philosophies on the earth not to be concerned with promoting balance on the planet. The conflicting ideologies presently in existence create tension and

King

stress, as is readily apparent. Any major rift or shift in human ideological tectonics could spell global disaster.

Mankind, in this Second Millennium, will now have to engage in the sacrificing of his individual (personal and national) needs and desires for the benefit of the whole (earth). Selfishness, self-centeredness, self-aggrandizement, self-proclamation and monarchy (the rule of one) simply will not work in this new era. They worked well and served their purpose during the last thousand years, but they will work no more. This is a new time . . . truly, demanding new and different thought from that which existed in the last millennium. Man's struggle now is to generate balance and create a sense of equilibrium between and among all people and nations of earth. He has had his time to conquer. It is now time for him to cooperate. This will be man's struggle for the next thousand years. He will have to learn to be at peace with his fellow man. If he doesn't, the consequences cannot and will not be favorable.

One thing needs to be mentioned here for clarity in relation to the 1 and 2 vibrations. Although '1' rules the male energy and, therefore, men in general, and the '2' rules the female energy and women in general, all of us, as exemplified in the Yin/Yang symbol, are a blend of masculine and feminine energies in various compositions. No person is comprised totally of all male energy or totally all female energy. In fact, the number 2 has more underlying masculine or 1 energy than any other number including the number 1 itself (see Chapter 3 – "Yin Power"). The point here – let's not jump on the bandwagon of gender. Placing weight on either end of the teeter-totter creates an imbalance deleterious to the highest and best good of the whole.

THE SHIFT IN VIEW

The Millennia Shift became noticeable in America in the 1920s with the political spotlight focused on the women's suffrage movement. After decades of struggle beginning in the mid Nineteenth Century, final ratification of the Nineteenth Amendment to the Constitution of the United States giving women the right to vote occurred on 26 August 1920. This amendment states: "The right of citizens of the United States to vote shall not be denied or abridged by the United States or by any States on Account of sex."

This modification, of course, opened the door for women to enter the entire judicial system, changing the face of the American electorate, and arguably the face of the world . . . forever. First gaining the right to vote, then entering the legal profession to become lawyers, judges, policy makers and leaders, women thus insured the expansion of the Yin. The cosmic clock was ticking in perfect time and souls were pulsating to its perfect rhythm. The seeds of a new age, a new millennium, had sprouted.

King

And what has the outcome of the suffrage movement been? Women are now integral to every facet of our society, filling corridors of commerce, art, aviation, athletics, finance, law, law enforcement, politics, communication, media, medicine, education and engineering. Such is the swinging of the Great Pendulum.

COSMIC COINCIDENCES

There are no coincidences in the universe. Whatever happens is destined to happen. Such is the divine law, a law manifested through numbers. The Millennia Shift is not a random happening but a construct of divine design.

Albert Einstein, preeminent scientist, Nobel Laureate in Physics and Time Magazine's Person of the Twentieth Century corroborates the concept of destiny:

> *Everything is determined, the beginning as well as the end by forces over which we have no control. It is determined for the insect as well as for the star. Human beings, vegetables or cosmic dust, we all dance to a mysterious tune intoned in the distance by an invisible piper.* (New York Academy of Sciences)

The 15th/16th Century mystic Guru Amardas states:

> *God himself forces his creatures into destined paths of karmas (fruits of previous actions) over which they have no control and which*

cannot be effaced. Whatever is destined to take place, must take place (qtd.in Singh 28).

Fascinating. Here we have the greatest scientific mind of the Twentieth Century and a revered mystic of the Fifteenth and Sixteenth Centuries averring the same fact of predestination. In fact, their language is practically identical! Einstein uses the phrase, *over which we have no control* and Amardas exclaims, *over which they have no control*. The only difference in these sentences is the use of the pronouns *they* and *we*. Science and mysticism, it seems, ultimately lead to the same source – wonderful food for sentient thought.

In thinking of this cosmic divine design to life, isn't it interesting that the women's suffrage movement, as a prime example of the Two energy in manifestation, was basically conceived in the Nineteenth Century and given birth through ratification of the 19th Amendment in the Twentieth Century (a 2 in vibration) and in the decade of the Nineteen Twenties (also a 2)!

Why is this interesting? Because in numerology One (1) represents the energy of the male, of action, creation and new beginnings. Nine (9) represents endings, conclusions, finalizations, the 'all,' the 'many,' the universal life stage. The number Nineteen (19) is a juxtaposition of the 1 cipher encompassing the 9 cipher of endings, thus creating new beginnings ($19 > 1 + 9 = 10 > 1 + 0 = 1$).

King

Furthermore, when the 1 is subtracted from the 9, the result is 8, the energy of social interaction and involvement. In this subtracted position the Eight (8) is referred to as a "challenge;" in this case denoting social disruption and disconnection. Thus, numerologically, the 20th Century with its 1900s base was a time of beginnings (1), endings (9) and bumpy goings (8) focusing on the development of a new social paradigm (1 and 8) involving the energy of the female.

The Number 19 Binary

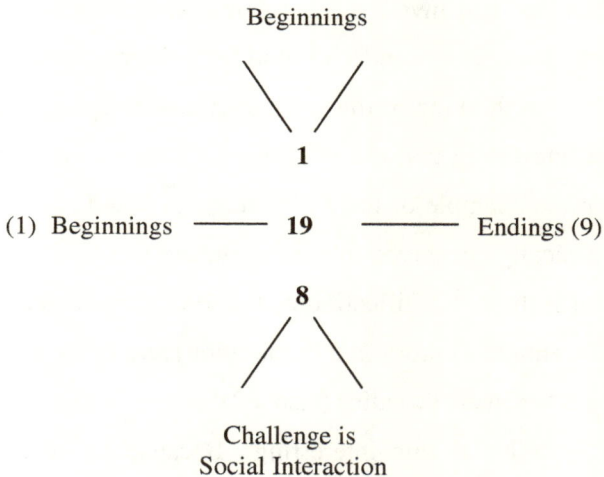

Beginnings

1

(1) Beginnings   ———   19   ———   Endings (9)

8

Challenge is
Social Interaction

And wasn't this the exact scenario our society faced during the Twentieth Century? The changes and challenges were basically social in nature. The world's population basically doubled in the last half of the Twentieth Century, growing from three billion people in

The Age of the Female: A Thousand Years of Yin

the 1960s to approximately six billion at the Millennia Shift. The entire world is now confronted with the threat of terrorism; personal data collection is massive; video surveillance is growing out of control; social diseases are threatening enormous numbers of people and countries, especially Africa with its AIDS epidemic; financial institutions (8 rules finance and commerce) have taken a huge hit with such scandals as Lincoln Savings (remember that fiasco) Enron and WorldCom, all of which have drastically challenged the financial security and well-being of countless individuals. These are all manifestations of the 8 Challenge derived from the 19 binary cipher.

Basically, with the number 19, its 1 Influence $(1 + 9 = 10: 1 + 0 = 1)$ and its 8 Challenge $(9 - 1 = 8)$, it's out with the old and in with the new. Social interaction, circulation and commerce are stressfully stimulated. Things end, conclude and come to resolution within the vibratory energy of the 9, while new things begin in the energy field of the 1 and are negatively aspected by the 8 in a challenge position. Specifically, during the last one hundred years, the male 1 energy underwent a phase of terminal resolution as our society underwent enormous challenges. In other words, during the Twentieth Century (the 9th century of the 1 millennium), the masculine vibration came to a close as the female energy rose in ascendance, i.e., the Age of the Female was in the birthing process (for further reading on the science of numbers see *The King's Book of Numerology, Volume 1, Foundations & Fundamentals*).

The 1900s (Twentieth Century) exhibited many extraordinary new beginnings juxtaposed with endings, which will be discussed later. The women's movement was simply one example. Are all these changes coincidence or cosmic science; happenstance or divine order?

Other major and specific signs of the previous millennium of the 1 giving way to the new millennium of the 2 are witnessed in part in the accomplishments of aviatrix Amelia Earhart, man's landing on the moon, the fall of the Berlin Wall, Title IX (American Education law regarding parity in female athletics), the life and death of Princess Diana of Wales, and the World Trade Center attacks of 911. The rise in popularity of divisive groups on a local and global level such as terrorists and gangs is also a benchmark of this period of millennia shifting, as is the business concept of 'networking,' which began taking noticeable shape during the 1980s.

MILLENNIUM AGING

The infancy/growth period of the Two Millennium will last approximately one hundred years. The first phase is from the year 2000 to 2009. During this initial phase, each of the basic nine numbers will be catalyzed and activated, one at a time.

The Age of the Female: A Thousand Years of Yin

2000 2001 2002 2003 2004

2005 2006 2007 2008 2009

The second phase will last ninety years as each number in succession (1-2-3-4-5-6-7-8-9) receives its own special decade (2010, 2020, 2030, 2040, 2050, 2060, 2070, 2080 and 2090). From the decade phase, the Second Millennium will proceed to her century (third) phase where each single number will be active for one hundred years. Such will be her life's journey. She will die on 31 December 2999, passing the cosmic torch to the Third Millennium and the Age of Self-Expression.

CORE ISSUES AND THEMES

The Age of the Female will have several major core issues possessing both positive and negative attributes. Just as we cannot hold a coin without holding both sides simultaneously, so we cannot experience a vibration without experiencing both of its polarities as well. It is the hope, of course, that mankind concentrates on the positive polarity because what man thinks, he becomes; what he plants, he sows; what he places on the circle, circles back to him. As Ravidas (a 15th/16th Century Saint) succinctly stated: *The fruit of action unfailingly overtaketh the doer*. Therefore, if we're going to be overcome, let us be overcome with balance, equilibrium, peace, joy, goodness, fairness, kindness, caring, cooperation, support, tenderness, love, generosity and grace. These are all positive aspects of the Female energy. Therefore, as she accedes and ascends to the throne for her cycle of cosmic rulership, let us all pray for her highest and best good and that she will become the apotheosis of the enlightened empress – the matriarchal, benevolent and quintessential queen of the millennium bearing her name and number.

The Age of the Female: Core Issues & Themes

Yin	Female	Women
Others	Relationship	Partnership
Togetherness	Support	Cooperation
Inspiration	Emotion	Intuition
Secrets	Hidden Knowledge	Hidden Agendas
Sensitivity	Insensitivity	Over-sensitivity
Receptivity	Kindness	Caring
Balance	Equilibrium	Harmony
Fairness	Indirectness	Vacillation
Duplicity	Duality	Deceit
Competition	Contention	Confliction
Rivalry	Tension	Polarization
Privacy Invasion	Self-absorption	Friendship

SUMMARY

Life is expressed in circles, cycles, sides and tides. In other words, everything has its time, place and purpose. In this temporal world nothing is forever. Energies come and go, as do periods of time. Indeed, to everything, including energy cycles and vibratory veils, there is a season, and cosmic seasons can be identified with numbers and their corresponding characteristics. These seasons, these periods of time, all have their reasons, as well as their purposes for being in the great and grand scheme of things. Nothing is without design. Everything has both purpose and place.

Owing to its polar paradigm, changes in this dimension are constant and certain, changes which can sometimes be trying and challenging due to dynamic shifts of diametrically opposed vibrational fields. Such a dramatic shift is the earth now experiencing as it moves into the energy field of the female 2 vibration and away from its antithetical polar male 1 counterpart.

To be sure, earth is no longer living within the energy field of the One – the male, the monarch and the pioneer. It is now living within the millennium of the Two – the realm of others, the female and her energy, the partner, the friend, helper, associate, assistant, accomplice, companion, collaborator, colleague, comrade, competitor, challenger, negotiator, diplomat, teammate, ally and adversary. It is also a time where balance and equilibrium will be critical to survival;

King

where emotion and intuition will find prominence and place; where kindness, caring, compassion and personal service will have more possibility of notoriety than ever before; where that which is hidden will be revealed; where reflection and illusion will wax, not wane; where that which lies on the surface may be opposite from that lurking beneath; where people may become self-absorbed and blind to the reality of others to the detriment of the whole; where forked tongues may be accepted and acceptable; where courage may find want and people may want for courage, and where the open, direct and straight truth may be overshadowed by the indirect shroud of duplicity and deceit.

Globally, governments must now take a new look at the 'cosmic' situation, as well as how to provide leadership in a world founded on thoughts of togetherness, partnership and positive personal interaction and association with others, as opposed to the qualities of oneness and self, which may have been necessary for the independence and survival of emergent and autonomous nations in the past, but which will neither serve nor promote the salutary interests of an emergent and autonomous world . . . a world which will not be marked as much by the pioneer as by the partner, a world challenged with promoting cooperation, not contention; accord, not discord; harmony, not inharmony; peace, not war; a world which will engender the well-being of others rather than serving the interests of the single self and . . . it will be a world which will not be so much a brave new world, but a new world in which we must all learn to be brave.

King

The Age of the Female: A Thousand Years of Yin

CHAPTER THREE

YIN POWER

In tradition it has been
that power rested with the men.
This thousand years will turn the tale
to a power base that is female.
Once was 'world' defined by man.
'World' is now defined by woman.
The masculine focus that has been,
has abnegated to the Yin.
As all things cycle, so does power.
Verily, within this hour
the cosmic clock confers . . .
the power now is hers.

Traditionally in numerology the number Two has been considered passive, a condition translating to weakness. Not true. The Two is more passive on its surface than its male One counterpart, but beneath its surface, the Two is dynamically rich in One energy, making Yin extremely powerful, assertive, creative, dynamic, inspirational, energetic, ego-driven

King

and self-oriented. The difference is that the power flowing from the Yin manifests *behind* the scenes and *below* the surface (the reason for its misinterpretation) while the One's power is openly visible above the surface.

Juxtaposing the numerical framework of the numbers One and Two reveals this fact. The top row is the *simple cipher* or *crown*. We can think of it as being "above the surface." The second row is the two digit *binary root*. The third row is the *transition root*. It is "below the surface."

The Number One: Root Chart

1	1	1	1	1	1	1	1	1	1
10	19	28	37	46	55	64	73	82	91
-	10	10	10	10	10	10	10	10	10

The Number Two: Root Chart

2	2	2	2	2	2	2	2	2	2
11	20	29	38	47	56	65	74	83	92
11	-	11	11	11	11	11	11	11	11

Notice the difference between the Ten (10) *transition roots* of the number One and the Eleven (11) *transition roots* of the number Two. *Transition Roots* rest below the surface of the single number and are the result of adding the two single numbers of the *binary*

The Age of the Female: A Thousand Years of Yin

roots together before being further reduced to a single digit, in this case the One and Two single ciphers.

In counting the number of ones in the entire transition root column of the number One, we find there are nine of them (each attached to a zero cipher as part of the number Ten). In contrast, there are eighteen ones in the transition root column of the number Two, twice as many as in the root system of the One! These are, of course, the eighteen ones forming the number Eleven in each of the transition roots. It is in this *transition root structure* of the Number Two where her power lies and which is responsible for her being "the power behind the throne," that is, behind the One in above-the-surface rulership. Remember the phrase, "behind every great man is a great woman?" This numerical configuration explains why this is so. As is clearly visible, the number Two is passive only on her surface. However, underneath her ostensibly passive veneer she is a powerhouse indeed! She may like to be hidden from view to the external world but her energy is dynamically and indirectly at work behind the scenes in the role of companion, partner, supporter, helper, divider, deceiver, agitator, adversary, peace lover or war monger.

The Two, therefore, although it has a reputation for being meek, is not. Quite the contrary. "Meek" does not equate to "weak." "Meek" is humble power. "Weak" is power challenged. They're very different words.

54

OBSERVATION: ONE vs. TWO

The juxtaposition of the One and Two root systems is as profound as it is revealing. The first thing it tells us is that with the number One there is a concentration of self-oriented energy above as well as below the surface. In other words, with masculine energy what you see is what you get. There is no hidden agenda. The manifestation is *direct*. What is on the outside is the same as that which is on the inside, albeit there is a saturation of self above and below.

However, the number Two energy gives a different perspective. First, there is a great deal of self-oriented energy in the Two vibration. The difference is that it lies underneath the surface and is hidden from view (viz. a viz. the Eleven (11) transition root structure). Although it doesn't show itself to the outside world directly, the Two is working diligently *indirectly*, behind the scenes.

The second thing is that in contrast to the One energy, what you see with the Two is not necessarily what you get and, in fact, is just the opposite of what you may be seeing! The surface expresses itself as a Two energy – passive, emotional, helpful, supportive, soft, tender, compliant, kind, caring, feminine, others and partnership oriented – all of which may be true. But the energy under the surface is active, assertive, aggressive, creative, independent and potentially harsh, hard and unyielding. This is the paradox of the number Two. It is passive on the outside and active on the inside. A good example of this would be undersea volcanoes – water above the surface but fire below!

It is this type of dual environment in which our civilization now finds itself. In the last millennium of the One, the environment was openly and directly distinguishable, for better or for worse. In this new age, nothing is clearly discernible. A contract, for example, may appear to be one way on its surface but its deeply buried fine print may tell a different story. This kind of deceit, unfortunately, is a negative aspect of Two energy now enveloping us.

There is no other shift between the single numbers One through Nine quite like this shift between the One and Two. No shift of opposites carries with it the immense fire of change than this pair. First, they are both filled with fire and ego. Second, they are still diametrically opposed to each other in their outer expressions. Third, they are as opposite as they can possibly be (One is masculine, Two is feminine; One is fire, Two is water; One is direct; Two is indirect). Yet, there is still more to add to the complexity of this millennia shift between the One and Two energies.

POLAR CHANGES

Here is another major factor as to why the Millennia Shift has been difficult. Each single number of the nine basic numbers maintains a polar charge of its own. All the odd numbers have positive charges; the even numbers, negative charges. The #9 is neutral because it houses both charges. See the following chart.

Polar Charges of the Basic Numbers

(odd numbers: positive; even numbers: negative)

1+   2-   3+   4-   5+   6-   7+   8-   9

When we apply these charges to the binary roots of the numbers One and Two, we get an interesting picture.

Binary Root Structure of the Number 1

(Each binary partner maintains the same charge.)

Binaries	+10	+19	-28-	+37+	-46-	+55+
Transition	10	10	10	10	10	10
Singles	+1	+1	+1	+1	+1	+1

Binaries	-64-	+73+	-82-	91+
Transition	10	10	10	10
Singles	+1	+1	+1	+1

Binary Root Structure of the Number 2

(Each binary digit except the 11 has an opposite charge)

Binaries	+11+	-20	-29	+38-	-47+	+56-
Transition	11		11	11	11	11
Singles	-2	-2	-2	-2	-2	-2

Binaries	-65+	+74-	-83+	92-
Transition	11	11	11	11
Singles	-2	-2	-2	-2

The Age of the Female: A Thousand Years of Yin

Here we see that each of the binary roots of the number One (10-19-28-37, etc.) maintain the same polar charge within each binary. For example, the binary root 37 is comprised of the single numbers 3 and 7, both of which have positive charges. The binary root 28 is comprised of the numbers 2 and 8, both having negative charges. The thing of note is that within each binary the charges of each single number forming that binary are identical. This means that no matter what the expression manifested, that expression will be direct and pure. What you see is truly what you get. There's no duplicity or confusion; no mixed messages or crossed signals. If it's negative, it's negative. If it's positive, it's positive.

However, in contrast to the One and its root structure, the number Two is very different. With the exception of the number 11, every binary root of the number Two is comprised of single numbers with opposite polarities! For example, the number 47 maintains a negative 4 charge and a positive 7 charge; the binary 38 houses a positive 3 charge and a negative 8 charge. As we see, the pattern is the same for the remaining binaries of the Two.

This polarized binary structure adds to the complexity of the number Two because even when something exists on the surface of its energy field, it carries both a positive and negative charge which creates possible confusion, duplicity, mixed messages and unclear signals. What is manifested will have some degree of opposition to it except in the case of a pure 11 vibration. In the number Two, positive and negative charges are forever waging a tug-o-war. This bi-polar binary structure is one which is vacillatory in nature. It explains in part why decisions are difficult to make under this vibration and why some people, for example, keep changing their minds – they sway from one polar charge to the other.

The great cosmic pendulum swings to and fro within the framework of the Two. No other single number has this type of binary root system. This is another reason why the Two is not only confusing but complex – it's filled with positive and negative energy in vacillation. Thus, the Two has the potential to flip-flop and change polarities in the blink of an eye. It can be loving one minute and hateful the next; greatly supportive in one moment and then extremely undermining, impeding and prohibitive in the next; complimentary on the one hand and critical on the other; hot and then cold; happy then sad, staunch advocate and then daunting adversary. These variances in extremes are why the Two energy sometimes seems unstable, inconsistent and emotional. Motion is movement, and when the pendulum sways back and forth from polarity to polarity with such ease and frequency it is easy for one to find himself in an emotional dilemma. Where one may consider himself bi-polar, perhaps he is not. It may

The Age of the Female: A Thousand Years of Yin

simply be the effect of the Two energy manifesting itself naturally – a numeric condition but not a medical one.

A corroborating difficulty for the Two is the conflict between its own external and internal energy fields – Two on the outside; One on the inside. Externally, the Two wants to follow and support but internally she wants to lead, create, dominate and take center stage.

The positive aspect of the Two's bipolar structure is that it maintains an ability to perceive and understand both sides of an issue, which is why the Two is the energy of diplomacy and interpersonal relationship. This intrinsic framework allows the Two to bend and adjust much more efficiently than the One which, because of its binary charge composition, has a difficult time bending and adjusting to other viewpoints. The One is, therefore, basically diplomatically challenged.

Another positive aspect of this bipolar energy of the Two is its intuition. Its perceptions are deeply sub-surface. This is why women, who are ruled by the number Two, are generally considered more intuitive than men (ruled by the number One).

In this Age of the Two, things hidden will now surface. Many mysteries, both positive and negative, will manifest and present themselves to a waiting world, creating challenges both dangerous and delightful.

With this explanation, hopefully one can see why the Millennia Shift is dramatic and why our new age is more complex than ever before. The world of the One has been totally ransacked, turned inside out and upside down. Simplicity has given way to multiplicity.

TENSION IN THE TWO

The inherent power of the Two is based in its Eleven root structure. Eleven (11) is known as a *master number* (double numbers of identical single digits: 11-22-33-44-55-66-77-88-99). The number Eleven is signified as the Master Aspirant/Achiever vibration because of its prominence in the charts of successful people. *Master numbers* are intrinsically intense. Although parallel in structure, they are unparalleled energetically, their power dual in potential (King 74-83; ch. 5).

The structure of the number Eleven reveals its profound secrets.

11

Here we see two Ones side by side, two separate entities – be they individuals, nations, cultures, ideas, ideals, ideologies, philosophies, viewpoints, genders – which may interact in a variety of ways. For example, they may be walking harmoniously hand-in-hand in the

The Age of the Female: A Thousand Years of Yin

same direction, sharing commonalties, enjoying and experiencing the warmth of togetherness and supportive compatibility, as in the following diagram.

**Separate individuals, ideals or ideas
in harmony and cooperation**

1↑↑1

On the other hand, they may be moving in opposite directions either on a vertical or horizontal plane, thus creating tug-o-war tension.

Opposite Moving 1s   Tug-O-War 1s

1↑↓1   ←1‑‑1→

Furthermore, they could be clashing, generating the tension of combat.

King

Clashing 1s

$$1\text{-}\!\blacktriangleright\!\blacktriangleleft\!\text{-}1$$

These entities, too, although they may be harmonizing, may be moving in a varied number of directions.

$$\leftarrow 1\ 1 \rightarrow$$

Partners may be sharing a reality of ascent, as well as descent; of moving far to the right or just as far to the left.

With all of these interrelated dynamics it is easy to see why the Eleven cipher (11/2) is packed with power and tension. Its high voltage energy is responsible for its inherent kindness, helpfulness, togetherness, inspiration, aspiration and achievement, but likewise, also for its contention, competition, adversity, interference, struggle, strain and stress. The master number Eleven is a pure representation of the dualistic forces operating in this creation. It is this energy with which all people on

The Age of the Female: A Thousand Years of Yin

the planet will have to deal for a thousand years. Like it or not, there is no way of escaping it. The trick is to learn to understand it, work with it, manage it, but not fight it.

The question at hand is: "Will mankind rise to the level of that which reflects the highest and best good of the Two, thereby creating a world of peace, compassion, harmony, justice, fairness and equality for all souls living on the earth, or will man be consumed by his own selfish wants, needs and desires, creating a world of war, a world waxing with clashing, conflict, contention and division?" Verily, these are opposing ideological constructs, both of which are quite valid. If we argue for our limitations, however, they will be ours, but if we likewise make claim to our highest and best good, they will be ours. We are what we think. We harvest what we plant. We reap what we sow. If we sow discord, we cannot harvest harmony, but if we sow harmony, it will be a wonderful harvest.

The choice is ours, of course, as to how we handle the power of the Yin, and we must inevitably choose, as one world, how we will handle that power, because, to be sure, we are one world now, or, better said, we need to be one world. With the kind of potentially destructive power now in the hands of so many countries and clusters of differing ideologies, it is far too dangerous a place not to be of one accord, at least in the issue of survival for our earth. Hopefully, as a race of human

King

beings, we will honor our elevation in the divine scheme of things and not forget that the consequences of our choices will become the fruit of the seeds we've planted, fruit we will be forced to consume either in joy or sorrow, laughter or tears, constructive love or destructive hate.

THE AGE OF BALANCE

The solution to conflict is balance; its result, peace. Ideally, the number Eleven depicts two Ones in perfect balance, the equalization of polar extremes and the hoped-for focus of this Second Millennium. Therefore, the Age of the Female – the Millennium of the Two – could and should also be called the Age of Balance.

Perfect Balance

The Spiritual Lesson for the Yin

How difficult is it, though, to balance and stay balanced? Ask anyone who has ever done a handstand, walked a tightrope or stood on one leg, especially with eyes closed. These are, of course, physical examples of balance, but it is just as challenging to create balance which is emotional, psychological, financial and

The Age of the Female: A Thousand Years of Yin

spiritual. Truly, balance is not an easy thing to master, which is why balance is a virtue. If everyone could do it, it would be easy and life for everyone would be good . . . very good, but it's not, so we struggle and keep trying, in spite of our failings and shortcomings.

When it is challenging to master balance on a personal level in all of its facets, how difficult is it then for a world to create balance, a world full of billions of souls, each with its own desires, wants, needs, likes, dislikes, drives, motivations, ideals, philosophies, prejudices, hates, envies, jealousies, opinions and agendas? Compound this by including separate nations in the mix, then conclaves of allies supporting common interests and the problem becomes extremely exacerbated, not to mention that most of us think we're right, others are wrong and they should adjust to us. Is it not true that we don't see things the way they are but the way we are? Such a reality underscores the difficulty our world now faces – critical thoughts for critical times.

Yet, there is hope. There is always hope. As a binary cipher, the number 11 is perfectly balanced in itself – a perfect image for each of us to hold within our mind's eye because the number 11 depicts equality between two 1s – be those 1s individuals, groups, nations, conclaves or consortiums. When balance is achieved, there is equality between opposing forces and peace is created.

King

The Number Eleven

11

Numerical Symbol of Perfect Balance

However, when there is no equality between opposing forces, imbalance is the result. Stability is compromised; problems arise; tensions are generated; egos wax and wane. Then the 1s get out of balance and the teeter-totter motion of instability begins. The result is often conflict, contention and war with all of its heartaches and attending evils.

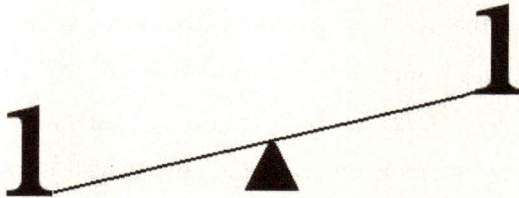

The goal, then, should be to work diligently to establish balance on a personal, national and global level because there can never be peace until there is balance.

The Age of the Female: A Thousand Years of Yin

1   The Goal
Separate entities in perfect balance   1

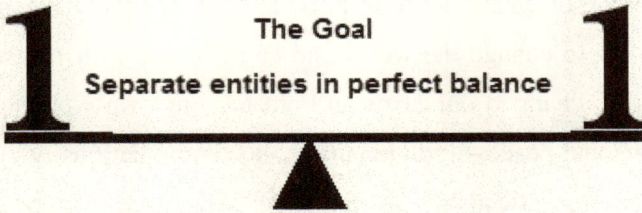

MICRO IN THE MACRO

There is no question the achievement of balance will be a major challenge for the world and its people throughout the next thousand years. This world perspective is the macro challenge. But how will the energies of this age affect the individual, the micro part of the macro whole? If the world is out of balance, does that mean each individual has to be? Of course not. In fact, the way to global peace is to find peace within ourselves individually first. Once we, the separate parts of the whole, are at peace, once we are balanced, then there is hope for the whole. But the process starts with the individual, the micro, not with the world, the macro. If we sit around and wait for the world to create peace before we create it in ourselves, we're in for a very long, long, long wait. Peace is created from the inside out, not from the outside in.

All spiritual teachings tell us that true peace can only come from within. We cannot look to the world for peace. Yet, how difficult is it to change ourselves, to find peace within ourselves, let alone change another person or create peace in him? How realistic is it, then, to try to change the world and create peace in it before we've changed ourselves and created our own world of personal peace – individually, collectively, nationally? It is not realistic at all. The best thing to do is light our own candle and do our best to increase its light rather than run around trying to light everyone else's candle at the risk of having ours extinguished by the wind we generate in our own ill-devised enterprises.

How do we create balance when dealing with an energy that is constantly shifting back and forth and doing its best to imbalance us? By first recognizing and then addressing the problem, realizing it is important to our personal well-being and that of the whole that we be proactive in working with the concept of balance. Balance is primary! By doing our individual part, the whole will be that much more enhanced, especially if we get our own egos in line and keep them checked by realizing that all of us are in the same boat, a boat that can and will sink if we're not careful. We can also help by knowing that no one in this world is really that much better than anyone else; that we all need each other now to survive and flourish and create a world which is safe and harmonious rather than unsafe and conflictive. If we do not get a handle on our egos and their selfish desires, wants and needs to the exclusion of other souls who inhabit this beautiful but tiny whirling sphere in the

The Age of the Female: A Thousand Years of Yin

distant reaches of the Milky Way, and they get out of control, we'll all be actors fit for a Shakespearean drama and, unfortunately, it will be a drama filled with tragedy, tribulation, heartache and tear-streaming sorrow.

On an individual basis, who are we anyway and how important are we to the whole? Do we think we are so important the world could not survive without us or that the world really cares about our accomplishments? If we think this way, we'd better get a grip on reality because we're harboring an unrealistic view of life. For example, who won the Nobel Peace Prize last year? Who won it for Literature? Physics? Chemistry? Medicine? Who was voted the man of the year? The woman of the year? The man or woman of the Twentieth Century? Most of us have little clue and could frankly care less. Let's face the truth – our lives revolve around us.

This is not a judgment. It is just an observation. But we must place ourselves in a proper perspective with other selves. It's okay to have needs and desires, but they cannot exceed or reach beyond the space and harmony of others. As the saying goes, "Your right to swing your fist ends where my nose begins." When we assert our own needs to the exclusion of others and their needs, the whole is thrown out of balance and then we have to fight to regain balance. In today's world, people don't fight with fists but bombs and other similarly destructive and nefarious weapons, weapons which have the potential of annihilating more than just a single nose.

King

Science has conferred there are more stars in the universe than all the grains of sand on all the beaches of the world. Therefore, how important can any of us truly be in the grand cosmic scheme of things even if we were king of the world? As Shakespeare said: "Uneasy lies the head that wears a crown" (*King Henry IV* 3.1.32). Reducing the size of our egos both personally and nationally cannot help but lessen global tension and its potential dangers.

SUMMARY

The Yin is extremely powerful. It is filled with both the energy of the female (manifested actively on its surface) and the male (active beneath its surface). These variances are, of course, depicted by the simple number 2 and its 11 transition root, a cipher which is highly energetic, nervous and high strung. The 11/2 vibration is teeming and beaming, flourishing and over-flowing with the positive energy of being involved with and helping others, supporting others and exploring the realm of others – other life styles, other points of view, perhaps even beings from other worlds. To be sure, in this Age of the Female there will be great focus on others and our relationships with them.

The 11/2 vibration is likewise filled with the energy of inspiration, supportive action, intensity, creativity, achievement, dialogue, tenderness, togetherness, partnership, cooperation, caring, kindness, diplomacy, balance, fairness, peace, equilibrium, intuition, passion and emotion. Reversing its side, the 11/2 maintains the energy of opposition, division, argumentation, separation, stress, tension, imbalance, instability, controversy, competition, confliction, vacillation, duplicity, deceit, jealousy, envy, unkindness, prohibition, interference, self-saturation, hidden agendas and war. Yet, in spite of this tension, both in its positive and negative forms, as we move ever forward into this new age, let us never forget the words of arguably the greatest statesman of the Twentieth Century, Winston Churchill: "Kites rise highest against the wind, not with it" (Brainyquote).

The Age of the Female: A Thousand Years of Yin

CHAPTER FOUR

NUMBER POWER

Numbers tell the time;
as well, they tell the tale;
numbers calculate the voyage
of life in its detail.

Numbers, just like coins,
incorporate two sides –
positive and negative,
as in the turn of tides.

Numbers are the codes of life;
they gauge, describe, define
the framework and the structure
of a life that is divine.

Numbers are life's basis
and, as cosmic law avers,
the blueprint of our destiny
has its design in numbers.

King

As discussed in the first chapter, numbers are the basis of our technological civilization. Without them society would collapse. Numbers are also the identifiers of specific attributes and characteristics for the framework of time and for the blueprint of every thing in existence, especially people and their destinies. Pythagoras was indeed right – numbers do rule the universe.

Nothing in creation is without design. The endeavors of the Twentieth Century were not happenstance. They were prodigiously powerful and prophetically portentous of the great changes dawning upon the earth. This chapter offers a brief numerological background for understanding the events shaping the new millennium.

KEYWORDS

Keywords are used in numerology to help identify the qualities and characteristics of numbers. There are thousands of individual words which can be used for each of the single ciphers 1 through 9, making it impossible to list every word associated with each number. However, it is possible to classify each of the simple numbers into nine categories.

The *Keywords Chart* below lists the ten binary roots of each single digit or *crown*. Notice, too, that each single number also maintains a *master number* in its binary structure.

The Age of the Female: A Thousand Years of Yin

As a side note, every single number maintains a positive and negative aspect. For example, the number One can be either self-confident or lacking in confidence; Two can manifest as war or peace; Three as health or disease; Four, construction or destruction; Five, freedom or slavery; Six, love or hate; Seven, the saint or sinner; Eight, integration or disintegration; Nine, benevolence or malevolence.

BASIC KEYWORDS CHART

ONE

Leader - Pioneer - Visionary

Binary Roots

10   19   28   37   46   *55*   64   73   82   91

Fire sign - symbol is the sun - Yang (male) - masculine - self - ego - identity - father - creator - initiator - activator - director - leader - authority figure - pioneer - independence - beginnings - active - dynamic - decisive - linear minded - single minded - logical - unique - original rational - rules reason - assertive - aggressive - courageous - strong - self-reliant - self-centered - solo - alone - maverick - lone wolf - oneness - union - yoga - willful - genesis - indivisibility.

TWO

Follower - Helper - Friend

Binary Roots

11 20 29 38 47 56 65 74 83 92

Water sign - symbol is the moon - Yin (female) - mother - the helper - supporter - partner - friend - team player - assistant - others - rules emotion - dependent - diplomatic - cooperative - considerate - kind gentle sensitive - receptive - reflective - responsive - intuitive - agreeable amenable patient - passive - peace making - equalizing rhythmic - reflecting - relationship - partnership - togetherness - duplicity - duality - deceit - competition - contention - vacillation - indecision - separation - tension - division - taking sides - self-saturation - impeding - interfering - inhibiting.

THREE

Communicator - Artist - Joy Giver

Binary Roots

12 21 30 39 48 57 *66* 75 84 93

Air sign - symbol is the triangle - golden mean - marriage - children - friends - joy - words - communication - self expression - health - sickness - disease - beauty - ugliness - modeling - image - vanity - art - pleasure - parties - fun - cheerful - optimistic - positive - social verbal - gregarious - imaginative - creative - glamorous - charming embracing - approachable - holistic - perfection seeking - critical

The Age of the Female: A Thousand Years of Yin

stern - harsh - vain - virtuous - sadness – sorrow - unhappiness - entitled - talkative.

FOUR
Organizer - Worker - Builder
Binary Roots

13 22 31 40 49 58 67 76 85 94

Earth sign - symbol is the square - framework - form - foundation - structure - stability - security - service - boundaries - routine - rules - roots - guidelines - order - organization - regimentation - restriction - limitation - work - effort - toil - matter - materialism - status quo - tradition - convention - discipline - confinement - commitment - job - construction and destruction - control - frugality - physical strength - stubbornness - practicality - fidelity - constancy - house - status quo - patterns - clerical - mechanical - operational - dutiful.

FIVE
Liberator - Messenger - Explorer
Binary Roots

14 23 32 41 50 59 68 77 86 95

Fire sign - symbol is wings - freedom - slavery - detachment - dissolution - accidents - change - movement - motion - mercurial - variety - diversity - versatility - shifts - senses - sensation - sensuality - wandering - exploring - experimenting - experiencing -

King

exuberance - enthusiasm - animation - multi-faceted - spontaneous - stimulation - adventurous - exhibitionist - animated - non-restrictive - footloose - free - wild - energetic - rebellious - volatile - mercurial - curious - revolutionary - unchained - flamboyant - non-conventional - travel - people - stimulation - liberation - uncertain - free-spirited - versatile - letting go - abhors reins and chains - Number of Man.

SIX

Nurturer - Homemaker - Lover

Binary Roots

15   24   *33*   42   51   60   69   78   87   96

Water sign - symbol is the heart - matters of love - family - domicile - domesticity - responsibility - adjustability - community - nurturing - nourishing - caring - empathetic - protector - provided - art - beauty - harmony - understanding - softness - giving - gentleness - warm - comfortable - personally loving - supporting - tolerant - responsive - addicting - addictive - hateful - cruel - jealous - envious - resentful - home and homeland.

SEVEN

Mystic - Student - Thinker

Binary Roots

16   25   34   43   52   61   70   79   *88*   97

Air sign - symbol is the shepherd's crook - analysis - introspection - reflection - internalization - separation - reclusion - seclusion - isolation - purification - perfection - poise - refinement - thought - study - wisdom - learning - mysticism - spirituality - religion - privacy - secrecy - investigation - curiosity - concern - chaos - stress - worry - trouble - turmoil - scandal - heartache - heartbreak - peace - bliss - tranquil - calm - inward moving - deep - distant - thoughtful - considerate - cool - cold - inquisitive - alone - withdrawing - sinners/saints.

EIGHT

Connector - Administrator - Executive

Binary Roots

17   26   35   *44*   53   62   71   80   89   98

Earth sign - symbol is the infinity symbol (lemniscate-sideways 8) - interaction - involvement - manipulation - connection - disconnection - circulation - circuits - circuitry - flow - coordination - continuation - comfort - administration - promotion - socialization - wealth - power - position - status - being in the loop - management - marketing - commerce - business - association - orchestration - organizer - externalization - organization - executor - execution - executive - leader -

King

conduit - pipeline - corporate - doer - mover and shaker - worldly success.

NINE

Thespian - Theologian - Humanitarian

Binary Roots

18   27   36   45   54   63   72   81   90   *99*

Grand Elemental (contains all signs) - symbol is the crown - ruler - macrocosm - humanitarian - philanthropist - public servant - healer - universal giver - philosopher - artist - theologian - thespian - public - travel - world - big picture - universal life stage - exposure - all-encompassing - drama - dramatic - tolerant - benevolent - malevolent - theatrical - dominant - domineering - expansive - broadcasting - endings - climaxes - finalizations - conclusions - resolutions - completions - terminations - the 'many' - the 'all' - Chameleon - generosity - understanding - intense emotion - crowds - the public spotlight.

THE BASIC MATRIX

The *Basic Matrix*, derived from a person's full name at birth and his birthdate, is a simple numerical blueprint of an individual and his destiny (King, ch.7). This seven-component tool will be invaluable in understanding the major players of The Age of the Female and the Millennia Shift.

The Age of the Female: A Thousand Years of Yin

The Seven Components of the Basic Matrix

	Component	Derivation
1	Expression	full name at birth
2	Lifepath	birth date
3	P/E: Performance/Experience	natal name plus birthdate
4	Soul (S)	vowels (a-e-i-o-u-y)
5	Material Soul (MS)	vowels plus birthdate
6	Nature (N)	consonants
7	Material Nature (MN)	consonants plus birthdate

The first three – Expression, Lifepath and Performance/Experience (P/E) comprise the *Umbrella* or outer world of a person's numerological chart. The *Expression* is the individual in all of his potentials, assets and liabilities and is derived from the full name at birth (natal name); the *Lifepath* is determined from the birthdate and literally describes the path a person is to follow during his life, attendant with all of its lessons and issues; the *P/E* (*Performance/Experience*) is the role/reality a person will experience as he traverses the path of his life. These three components can also be interpreted as the Actor (Expression) reading a Script (Lifepath) and giving a Performance (PE). See the following flow chart.

King

When an

ACTOR

(Numerology label: Expression)

(Derived from the Natal Name)

Reads a

↓

SCRIPT

(Numerology label: Lifepath)

(Derived from the Birth date)

He gives a

↓

PERFORMANCE

(Numerology label: PE or Performance/Experience)

(Derived from adding the Expression to the Lifepath)

The remaining four components of the Basic Matrix constitute the *inner core*. They are the Soul, Material Soul, Nature and Material Nature.

The *Soul* is derived from the vowels of the natal name of a person. It defines his basic needs, wants, desires and motivations. The Soul is the fire in the belly. Hidden from view to the outside world, it is the driving force in a person's life. The appellation *soul* is not the spiritual soul of God contained in every person but rather a simple word used in numerology to describe the centerpoint or *core* (soul) of an individual.

The Age of the Female: A Thousand Years of Yin

The *Material Soul* is derived from the addition of the Soul and the Lifepath. It describes how the basic Soul will manifest in the material world.

The *Nature*, derived from the consonants in the natal name, defines the individual's personality and manner in which he goes about doing things. The *Material Nature* describes the energy field in which the Nature plays itself out in the material world.

CALCULATING THE COMPONENTS

Calculating the numerical value of each of the seven components of the Basic Matrix is easy. All we have to do is add numbers together. Every component except the Lifepath will have letters attached to it, letters which have to be converted to a numerical value before we can apply meanings (keywords) to the components. Below is the *Basic Letter Value Chart*. It shows the single number value of every letter. Notice that letters form groups. A-J-S all maintain a single value of 1. B-K-T all have a value of 2; C-L-U have a 3 value and so forth.

Basic Letter Value Chart

A	B	C	D	E	F	G	H	I
J	K	L	M	N	O	P	Q	R
S	T	U	V	W	X	Y	Z	
1	**2**	**3**	**4**	**5**	**6**	**7**	**8**	**9**

To transform a name into its most basic numerical equivalent, we simply write down the name, place the corresponding numerical value below each letter, add the numbers left to right and reduce to a single digit. Thus, the name "John Doe" would be as follows:

Letters	J	O	H	N	D	O	E
Numbers	1	6	8	5	4	6	5

$$= \quad 35 \quad > \quad 8$$

John Doe's *Expression* is an Eight (8). We would then consult the Keywords Chart under the number 8 to glean a cursory view of who John Doe is. We would follow this simple format for the *Soul* (vowels) and *Nature* (consonants). To determine the *Material Soul* and *Material Nature*, we simply add each of their single ciphers to the single cipher of the *Lifepath* (its calculation below).

The simple *Lifepath* is computed in the same way. Giving John Doe a birthdate of 9 March 2002, we simply place the numbers of his date of birth on a horizontal line, add left to right and reduce to a single digit, just like we did with the Expression.

$$9 \; + \; 3 \, (\text{March}) + 2002 = 16 > 1 + 6 = 7.$$

Therefore, John Doe's Simple Lifepath is a 7. To ascertain the path J.D. will travel in life and the lessons

The Age of the Female: A Thousand Years of Yin

(both positive and negative) he will be learning, we cross-reference the 7 with the keywords chart.

J.D.'s role in life (PE) is discovered by adding his 8 Expression to his 7 Lifepath, the result being a 6.

8 Expression + 7 Lifepath = 6 PE.

THE LIFE MATRIX

The *Life Matrix* is the superstructure of the *Lifepath* and addresses the separate components of an individual's journey through life, describing the energy fields to be traversed, their timelines, influencing characteristics and outcomes.

There are three major components to the *Life Matrix*: 1) *Epochs*; 2) *Pinnacles* and 3) *Challenges*. Like the *Basic Matrix* components, each of these three components will be used to reference the major players and events of the Second Millennium.

As the *Lifepath* is the script/screenplay of a person's life, the *Epochs* can be likened to acts; the *Pinnacles* and *Challenges* to the scenes of the play, the drama.

There are three epochs in the *Life Matrix*, each corresponding to the day, month and year of a person's birth. For example, in John Doe's birthdate of 9 March 2002, his first *Epoch* is 9, his second *Epoch* is 3 and his final or third (Crown) *Epoch* is a 4 (2002 in reduction).

The *Pinnacles* and *Challenges* (which share the same timeline) are derivatives of the Epoch components through both addition and subtraction (Pinnacles by addition; Challenges by subtraction). There are four Pinnacle/Challenge sets. The periods of time during which the Epochs, Pinnacles and Challenges are active vary in length. The Third P/C couplet (Pinnacle/Challenge set), also known separately as the Grand Pinnacle/Challenge couplet, is referred to as the *core* of the Lifepath, just as the *Soul* is the *core* of the individual. This is because it carries tremendous power in the destiny.

Epochs, Pinnacles and Challenges comprise the *Life Matrix* (Lifetime Table). The diagram below shows the basic Epoch, Pinnacle and Challenge format. The second diagram is the same schematic using John Doe's birthdate of 9 March 2002.

Please note there is much more depth to numerology than the previous discussion offers. However, it should be sufficient for our needs at this time and is given simply to satisfy any curiosity as to how the basics of numerology work. For a deeper understanding of the Life Matrix, the Epochs, Pinnacles and Challenges, please refer to *The King's Book of Numerology II – Forecasting, Part 1.*

LIFE MATRIX

Add to generate Pinnacles; Subtract for Challenges

4th/Crown
Pinnacle

3rd/Grand
Pinnacle

1st   2nd
Pinnacle   Pinnacle

1st   2nd   3rd
Epoch   Epoch   Epoch
(Day)   (Month)   (Year)

1st   2nd
Challenge   Challenge

3rd/Grand
Challenge

4th/Crown
Challenge

King

LIFE MATRIX
John Doe: Born 9 March 2002

4

1

3   7

9   3   4

6   1

5

5

Let's now continue our fascinating journey into the Age of the Female by looking at the profound events of the Twentieth Century, the 1900s, and how they were prophetically and powerfully foretold through numbers.

C H A P T E R F I V E

APPROACHING SIGNS I

A hundred years before the Shift
symbols, ciphers, signs appear,
casting shadows over all –
the Morrow drawing near.

The day awakens with the dawn;
seamless transits bring new light;
the day retires with the dusk –
seamless shifts to night.

But shifts do bring their shadows
cast by portents on the rise,
fading with the noon-day sun
in a panoply of surprise.

Nothing is without design;
storms and seasons have their schemes;
in a world of illusion,
nothing is as it seems!

King

As this new Age of the Female approached, and particularly in the hundred years before it (the 1900s of the Twentieth Century), there were symbols, ciphers and signs being deposited and deployed all around us without our knowing in the form of major world events; symbols, ciphers and signs woven into the fabric of the great cosmic drama of planet earth; symbols, ciphers and signs acting both as hallmarks of the Twentieth Century and harbingers of the millennium to come; symbols, ciphers and signs defining, describing, acknowledging and proclaiming the divine design of all things. The construct of these events took the form of number and mathematical shape just as Pythagoras averred, and there were so many of these portentous cosmic cryptograms that anyone possessive of a clear, unbiased and scientific mind would be greatly challenged not only to deny them but to deny the existence of an indescribable, infinite, intelligent power creating them.

Judgments in a court of law are usually decided on a preponderance of evidence. The evidence that a design exists to our lives and destinies, even the life and destiny of earth, is here laid before you for you to decide. Is life happpenstance, or is life a construct of symbols, ciphers and signs? Was the Twentieth Century a time period of transition and shift between the 1 and 2 energies of the 1st and 2nd Millennia culminating in a new age and a new time, or was it just a random happening without

The Age of the Female: A Thousand Years of Yin

order, without design, without meaning, without mystery? You be the judge.

THE EVENTS

The Number 19

The first symbol, cipher and sign of note is the number 19, which we have already discussed, where the singular energies of the male and the self (1) were coming to a close (9), creating a new order (1 addcap) and challenged with social upheaval and readjustment (8 subcap) as reflected in not one but two world wars and a cold war, massive civil rights movements in America and India, political and ideological defiance as reflected in the counter-culture of the Sixties, and the emergence of terrorism on a global scale as witnessed by occurrences in the Middle East and the first of two World Trade Center bombings in America, the second, of course, ending in total disaster on September 11th of 2001 – just cosmic nanoseconds after the Millennia Shift. Indeed, the social order was changing . . . and none of it was comfortable. Things were ending. Things were beginning. Polarities were reversing. The world was being turned inside-out and upside-down and her people, for better or worse, had to contend with it all.

Why all this confusion? Because a new cosmic energy was fast approaching, its emergence inevitable. Such an energy would have to be addressed and

King

embraced, an energy the world had never known in toto before. That energy, of course, was the energy of the 2, the energy of the female and others, and, as we shall soon see, it is a numerical vibration overflowing in the charts of the main players and events of the Twentieth Century.

The Population Explosion

In order for the world to be involved with others, there have to be a lot of others for the world to be involved with. The population explosion of planet earth during the Twentieth Century created a world of others unlike anything previously witnessed in the recorded history of mankind.

Estimates are that in the year 1000 the population of earth was approximately 254 million people. In 1800 there were 813 million, an increase of only 559 million people in a timespan of eight hundred years. Not a very dramatic increase, to say the least. Thus, for most of the last millennium, the population of planet earth was fairly static and stable. However, as the energy of the 2nd Millennium began approaching and its light began to dawn upon mankind in the Twentieth Century, things began to shift and grow dramatically.

By the year 1900, the world population swelled from 813 million (in 1800), to 1.5 billion – an increase of 687 million people (U.S. Census Bureau, World Population). This increase was larger than that of the entire eight hundred year period preceding it – from the year 1000 to 1800 – a remarkable increase.

But the world population increase from 1800 to 1900 was just the tip of the emerging iceberg. Only a century later, the population of planet earth virtually exploded, quadrupling from 1.5 billion (1900) to 6 billion in the year 2000! This is a 300% increase in world population in just one hundred years! Furthermore, estimates are that by the year 2050, the population of earth will be 9 billion people (U.S. Census Bureau, Midyear Population). This figure, if accurate, will represent a sextupling 500% increase in world population in the brief time period of only one hundred and fifty years! Truly, the energy of 'others' came roaring in like a lion and crashing the shoreline of human existence like a tidal wave of immense proportions. See the following chart.

King

General population estimates from the year 1000 to 2050.

Year	Number
1000	254 million
1100	301 million
1200	360 million
1300	360 million
1400	350 million
1500	425 million
1600	545 million
1700	600 million
1800	813 million
1900	1.5 billion
2000	6.0 billion
2050	9.0 billion

To understand this dramatic, even staggering change in our world's population, the following graph offers a visual representation of the people boom. When looking at it, one almost gets the impression of a rocket blasting off from earth, and in fact that's a good representation of what happened number wise – the world population blasted off and rocketed into the new frontier of the Female Age.

Estimated Population Growth: 1000 to 2050 (est.)

Estimated Population Growth: 1000 to 2050 (est.)

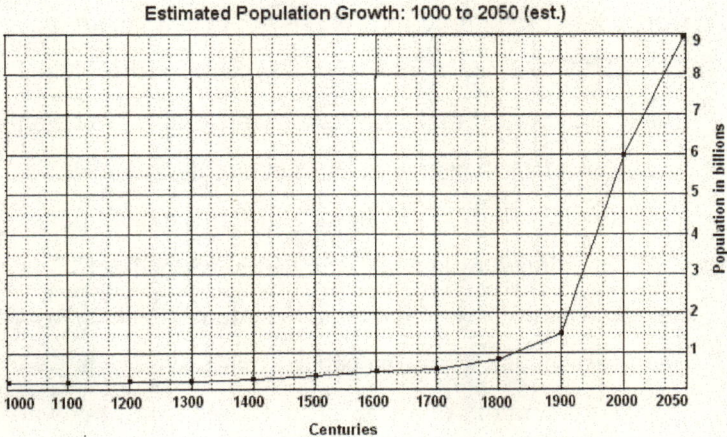

Centuries

The question is now begged. How does the world population increase so drastically in such a short amount of time? Is it simply a mathematical progression? If it were, there wouldn't be such an extraordinary disparity in the world population growth curve as there is. No. There's something else. That something else is energy – invisible, silent, cosmic-spiritual energy in ascendance, an approaching vibrational tidal wave so massive and powerful that *it* compels the changes we experience in and on the earth. It is this 2 wave of vibratory energy and essence that is cause. Everything else is effect . . . from the population explosion of planet earth to women in power to divisions of ideologies. Strange? Maybe. Unbelievable? Maybe. Totally off the wall? Maybe. But if it's not this spiritual-cosmic energy, then what is it? Something's causing these changes and it's certainly not the density of the bedrock in Montana.

King

The Women's Suffrage Movement

Probably no other single event of the Twentieth Century foreshadowed the Age of the Female more than that of the women's suffrage movement in the United States during the mid Nineteenth and early Twentieth Centuries. This movement, of course, gave women the right to vote and therefore make a difference in all things earthly – something that women had never had before in the recorded history of mankind. The female energy was on the ascent and it was, indeed, a remarkable event.

In that era of American history, votes meant power and with power in hand, woman and women could now influence public policy. As time marched on, woman would make policy. Furthermore, her influence will continue to make policy as her energy impresses itself more deeply into the vibrational infrastructure of the 2nd Millennium. This quickening of the female spirit will continue to affect human kind throughout the world. It is quite definitely with us to stay . . . at least for a thousand years.

Popular consensus is that the women's suffrage movement actually began in the middle of the Nineteenth Century at the Seneca Falls Women's Rights Convention in July of 1848, organized by Elizabeth Cady Stanton and Lucretia Mott (Seneca Falls Convention). It was at this convention that giving women the right to vote was seriously considered. From that point in time, and for the next seventy years, women would fuel and refuel the fires of political equality. It was not an easy struggle. Entrenched mindsets of masculine solidity held dear by both men and women had to be readjusted. Finally, with continued perseverance and by instatement of the 19th Amendment to the Constitution of the United States on 26 August 1920, women were guaranteed the right to vote. That Amendment reads:

> *The right of citizens of the United States to vote shall not be denied or abridged by the United States or by any States on Account of sex. The Congress shall have the power by appropriate legislation to enforce the provisions of this article* (National Archives, 19th Amendment).

With the new tide of the 2nd Millennium and its female energy fast approaching during the 1900s, one would expect to see numerical indications of woman ascending the steps of the world's throne to take her place along side her already established male counterpart. And so it was. And because, as Pythagoras declared, *Numbers rule the universe. Everything is arranged according to number and mathematical shape*, one would expect to see symbols, ciphers and signs of her approach reflected in numbers and especially in the number 2 and its binary root the number 11. And so this was as well.

The 19th Amendment was an example of this ascendancy. Prophetically, it occurred in the Twentieth Century (20 is a 2 vibration) during the Twenties decade of that century (the 1920s, obviously a 2 influence). Furthermore, the General Expression of the word *suffrage* is a 38/11/2 vibration!

```
S   U   F   F   R   A   G   E
1   3   6   6   9   1   7   5   >   38   3+8 =   11/2
```

As if more corroborative evidence were needed to validate the reality of numbers as they manifest themselves on the great life stage, Elizabeth Cady Stanton, generally regarded as one of, if not the main catalyst of the women's suffrage movement, and who was born on 12 November 1815 (Banks), had a Lifepath of 38/11/2 (same vibratory pattern as the word *suffrage*), an 11/2 Material Nature, a Core Challenge PE of 11/2 and a Crown Challenge PE of 11/2! Ms. Stanton's life and destiny were saturated with female energy. Her life lessons, personality and the primary challenge, as well as the ending challenge of her life, were all concentrated within the energy field of the Yin. Coincidence?

Such a 'coincidence' of the 11/2 cipher between Elizabeth Cady Stanton and the women's suffrage movement is not uncommon. In fact, such numerical

The Age of the Female: A Thousand Years of Yin

'coincidences' keep appearing during many of the events of the 1900s, thus forcing one to reflect on the reality of numbers as they relate to life and its manifestations.

Television

How important is the television to the modern world? Who would want to do without it? Who could do without it? For the world of 'others' to be fully enveloped and developed, there must be a way of bringing all people together. Enter the television.

Like the women's suffrage movement, which culminated in the Twenties decade of the Twentieth Century, the history of the development of television has clear roots in the 1920s. Although many scientists and inventors were responsible for the development of the television, John Logie Baird, a Scotsman born on 13 August 1888 (Wikipedia), began perfecting a machine designed to transmit moving images. He had successfully demonstrated these in what were called 'shadowgraphs' in 1925, and on 23 January 1926 he gave the world's first public demonstration of a mechanical television apparatus to approximately forty members of the Royal Institution at his laboratory. These were images of living human faces, not outlines or silhouettes, with tonal gradations of light and shade (Television History). Thus, the age of television, of communicating with others viz. a viz. actual moving images, was

100

anchored. Its growth from that time forward needs no explanation.

What is numerologically exciting, is that John Logie Baird, like Elizabeth Cady Stanton, had 11/2 energy is his chart. His birthdate of 13 August 1888 manifests a Crown Pinnacle of 38/11/2, which was also the Specific Lifepath of Stanton. His Second Epoch PE was an 11/2, as was his Second Challenge PE.

Flight

Because the tidal wave of the Yin and 'others' was fast approaching during the Twentieth Century, there needed to be some physical way to connect all of the 'others' around the world. The number 2, as we know, is not a lone wolf number on its surface, although its underlying 11 energy is quite individualistic. The number 2 is the first vibration of interpersonal relationship. How would the world become connected in such a way that involvement with 'others' became more physically personal? The answer: flight. Enter the Wright Brothers, Charles Lindbergh and Amelia Earhart.

Wilbur and Orville Wright invented and built the first successful airplane. They had been expending efforts to develop a power-driven, heavier-than-air machine since 1900, and on 17 December 1903, near Kitty Hawk, North Carolina, they became successful. Their airplane flew a distance of one hundred twenty feet and was airborne for twelve seconds (Couteau, First

The Age of the Female: A Thousand Years of Yin

Flight). Thus, the reality of travel by air began. It would, of course, be years before the first commercial airliner was operational but, nonetheless, airplanes now existed and modern man could fly, soar and interconnect with others around the world.

Wilbur Wright was born on 16 April 1867 (Couteau, Wilbur). His Material Nature was an 11/2; his 1st Pinnacle was an 11/2; his Crown Pinnacle was an 11/2 and his 1st Challenge PE was an 11/2.

Orville Wright was born on 19 August 1871 (Couteau, Orville). His Natural Soul Urge was an 11/2; his 1st Challenge was an 11/2 and his Grand and Crown Challenges were both 2s. The fact that both of the Wright Brothers had so much 2 energy in their numerology charts is not unusual because both were highly involved in the same work, sharing the same vision. Therefore, they would have to have similar energies in their charts. The fact that they were siblings could not but help further the advancement and inter-personalization of mankind by air travel.

To add to their 2 energy similarities, the date 17 December 1903 – the day of their first successful heavier-than-air flight, maintained an 29/11/2 1st Pinnacle! The name "Kitty Hawk," the place of their flight, was a 38/11/2! Interestingly, "Kitty Hawk" begins and ends with the letter "K" – the 11th letter of the alphabet. With the Wright's work, the process of globally connecting 'others' began. Isn't it interesting how events

King

and people are so intricately and numerically connected? Is this happenstance or cosmic design?

Transatlantic Flight

Charles Augustus Lindbergh Jr., 'Lucky Lindy' as he came to be known, was born on 4 February 1902 (Wikipedia, Lindbergh) – the same time frame in which the Wright Brothers were developing their airplane. It was Lindbergh, however, who would do what no man had ever done – fly a plane solo across the formidable Atlantic Ocean.

His heroic feat began on 20 May 1927 (a 2 calendar day). With a few sandwiches and a couple canteens of water, he took off from Roosevelt Field, Long Island, New York, at 7:52 A.M. in his plane, the 'Spirit of St. Louis.' Thirty-three and a half hours later on 21 May at 5:22 P.M. (New York time) he landed at Le Bourget Field near Paris, France – a distance of some thirty-six hundred miles – to an awaiting crowd of one hundred thousand people. Charles Lindbergh was an instant global hero at the tender young age of twenty-five. For this accomplishment, President Calvin Coolidge honored him with the Congressional Medal of Honor (the highest award for valor in the United States) and for valor while flying, the Distinguished Flying Cross. New York City also honored him with the largest ticket-tape parade in history (Ranfranz).

The Age of the Female: A Thousand Years of Yin

Lucky Lindy, the lone wolf, had brought the people of America and Europe together. His solo transatlantic flight came just seven short years after women's suffrage was attained with the passage of the 19th Amendment. The Age of the Female and the Age of Others was taking solid shape.

The 2s in the chart of Charles Lindbergh: 1st Challenge; 2nd Epoch. He also had an 11/2 Grand Pinnacle (the core of his 9 Lifepath) and an 11/2 Crown Pinnacle PE. The 'Spirit of St. Louis' also hosts a 74/11/2 Expression. How fitting it is that the airplane that spanned an ocean and brought the people of Europe and America together should also get in on the act, the act of expressing the 2 energy of service to others. The number Two definitely ties and binds.

Yin Flight

Yin must not be outdone, especially by Yang, and especially in the Twenties Decade of the Twentieth Century when the Wind of Woman was passionately approaching, swiftly wafting on waxing wings in the cosmic heavens. Enter Amelia Mary Earhart, aviatrix, born on 24 July 1897 (Wikipedia, Earhart).

Amelia Earhart was a woman of her time, before her time, in the time of Yin ascendance where women usually didn't do the daring deeds or have the 'daring do' of men. Earhart, a tomboy at heart, had grit . . . and lots of it. A woman of strong conviction, she fell in love with airplanes while attending a stunt-flying exhibition with one of her friends. The arrow of a winged cupid hit its mark, and on 28 December 1920, a pilot named Frank Hawks gave her the life-changing airplane ride of her life. "By the time I had got two or three hundred feet off the ground," she said, "I knew I had to fly." Within six months she managed to buy her own airplane, a two-seater biplane which she named Canary and in which she broke the women's altitude flight record on 22 October 1922 when she rose to 14,000 feet.

Then, on an April afternoon in 1928 she received a telephone call querying her as to whether she would like to fly the Atlantic. She jumped, or rather flew, at the chance. Flying with pilot Bill Stultz and co-pilot/mechanic Louis E. 'Slim' Gordon, she left Trepassey Harbor, Newfoundland, in a Fokker F7 on 17 June 1928. Twenty-one hours later she and her two male flight companions landed at Burry Port, Wales. Amelia Mary Earhart, less than one month shy of her thirty-first birthday, became the first female to fly across the Atlantic Ocean. Within one year, Yin and Yang had now physically spanned the airways and waterways between Europe and America. The tapestry of global interpersonalization was being woven both via the male (1) and female (2) forms.

Amelia Earhart was a true pioneer and set many records in aviation. On 20-21 May 1932 (beginning on a 2 calendar day) she became the first woman to fly solo

The Age of the Female: A Thousand Years of Yin

across the Atlantic. This was on the 5th Anniversary of Lindbergh's flight. She did this in 14 hours and 56 minutes. For her heroics she was awarded the National Geographic Society's gold medal from President Herbert Hoover, and Congress awarded her the Distinguished Flying Cross. On 11 January 1935 (a 2 calendar day) she became the first person, not just woman, to fly solo across the Pacific Ocean, a journey of 2,408-miles between Honolulu and Oakland, California (Earhart). When one thinks about it, this was an absolutely amazing accomplishment. "Hooray" for the daring do of Yin!

The number 2 appearing in the chart of Amelia Earhart: an 11/ 2 Lifepath; 11/2 1st Pinnacle PE and an 11/2 Crown Pinnacle PE.

<u>Satellite Flight</u>

Sputnik. The very word sent chills of fear into the heartland of America. Why? Because *sputnik* was the first artificial satellite to orbit the earth, launched by the USSR (Union of Soviet Socialist Republics) in 1957. The Soviet Union, with its Communist ideology, was America's arch rival and Cold War adversary and so thoughts of military domination and defeat loomed frighteningly large throughout America. If the Soviet Union, whose leader, Nikita Kruschev, said "we will bury you," got the upper hand in space, then Americans believed the fate of the free world would be at risk.

Therefore, with the launching of *Sputnik*, the space race was on, and the space age began in a flurry and fury of fright and foreboding.

Sputnik, whose Expression is a 29/11/2, was launched on 4 October 1957. Weighing only one hundred eighty-three pounds, it was approximately the size of a basketball and took about ninety-eight minutes to orbit the earth (Sputnik). It was, indeed, a scientific marvel for mankind. America's leap into space began on 31 January 1958 when she successfully launched her own artificial satellite, Explorer 1.

One of the prophetic photos during this race-to-space era can be found on the National Air and Space Museum website. It depicts two national rockets and their astronauts, American and Russian, standing side by side in the form of the number 11 (NASM, fig 1)! It is a perfect example of how symbols and images reflect the reality of the times.

Although military might was arguably a prime motivation in early satellite development, the utilization of its technologies would eventually serve to shrink the world by creating an outerspace communications network of hundreds of satellites. In fact, without the satellite and the technology which was developed as a result of the space race, we wouldn't have digital watches, cell-phones, satellite dish television, weather forecasting, the global positioning system (GPS), and all of the services they render to mankind.

The Age of the Female: A Thousand Years of Yin

Dr. William Ailor, Ph.D., Director of the Center for Orbital and Reentry Debris Studies with The Aerospace Corporation, says that in the year 2002 there were no less than 700 operating satellites circling the earth and about 10,000 man-made objects in orbit consisting of dead satellites, debris from explosions, rocket bodies and other space junk. Those that are tracked are generally larger than a basketball (Ailor).

Therefore, satellite flight, which began with a mini globe named *sputnik* circling the theater of our globe and infusing fear into the hearts and minds of Americans, had a silver lining, the lining of increased communications capability for the whole world. This, of course, eventually translated into more modern conveniences for the people of earth, enriching their lives, increasing their standard of living, maximizing business efficiency and, without a doubt, generating a consciousness of 'others' as never before.

Space Flight

Just as the Russians were the first to place an artificial satellite around the world, they were also the first country of the Cold War to place a man and a woman in orbit. The man – Yuri Gagarin; the woman – Valentina Tereshkova.

Yuri Alexeyevich Gagarin, born on 9 March 1934, became the first reputed human being to escape the gravity of earth in the spaceship Vostok 1 on 12 April

1961. He was 27 years old. At a speed of 18,000 miles per hour, Vostok 1 and its precious human cargo orbited the earth one time at an altitude of nearly 188 miles for 108 minutes. As the Genoan explorer Christopher Columbus proved the world was round during his voyage to the new world in 1492, Yuri Gagarin proved it visually during his space voyage to the new world of space in 1961 – 469 years later (Gagarin).

Soviet cosmonaut Valentina Vladimirovna Tereshkova was born on 6 March 1937. As Amelia Earhart was the first woman to fly across the Atlantic, Tereshkova was the first reputed female to fly across, not just the Atlantic, but every ocean of the world. This first woman in space was launched in the space capsule Vostok 5 on 16 June 1963. Lasting nearly three days, Tereshkova, at age 26, orbited the earth 48 times (Tereshkova).

The first American in space was Alan Bartlett Shepard Jr., born 18 November 1923. His Mercury space capsule, Freedom 7, lifted off from Cape Canaveral, Florida, on 5 May 1961. Prior to launch there were some technical difficulties to which he radioed his launch center: "I'm cooler than you are. Why don't you fix your little problem and light this candle!"

Folklore now established, eventually the candle was lit, not just on his Redstone missile, but on the American space program, and Alan B. Shepard was rocketed into space for a quick hop of fifteen minutes at a peak altitude of 116 miles before he touched down in the Atlantic Ocean. Although not a long flight, it was the first space flight for America, and Shepard's slingshot ride was notice to the Soviet Union that the United States had entered the space race (Shepard).

The first American woman in space was Sally Kristen Ride, born on 26 May 1951. The gap between the first acknowledged Soviet man and Soviet woman in space was only two years. America was more cautious. It would be approximately twenty-two years before Sally Ride was launched into space as part of the shuttle Challenger (STS-7) mission in 1983 (Ride).

The numbers of these four courageous space pioneers indicate the same vibrational influences we have already seen heretofore. Their charts are all loaded with 11/2 energy! Regardless of nationality, the cosmos does not play favorites. Numbers are not politically, ethnically, sexually, geographically, philosophically or religiously specific. Numbers and their vibrations are universal, blind to nationality, sexuality and ideology.

Following are the 11/2 vibrations occurring in the charts of these four human space explorers and pioneers.

Yuri Alexeyevich Gagarin, born 9 March 1934: First acknowledged human in space: 11/2 Lifepath; 11/2 2nd Pinnacle; 11/2 Grand Pinnacle PE; 11/2 2nd Challenge PE; 22 in his fourth house.

Valentina Vladimirovna Tereshkova, born: 6 March 1937: First acknowledged female in space. 11/2 Lifepath and 11/2 Expression.

Alan Bartlett Shepard Jr., born 18 November 1923: First American male in space: 11/2 1st Pinnacle; 11/2 First Pinnacle PE; 11/2 2nd Epoch; 11/2 2nd Epoch PE.

Sally Kristen Ride, born 26 May 1951: First American female in space: 11/2 Lifepath; 11/2 Nature; 11/2 2nd Challenge; 11/2 1st Epoch PE.

What these numbers also show is that the number 2, normally regarded as passive in traditional numerology, is not really passive at all. It is very active and courageous. How could all of the foregoing accomplishments be realized by passive souls? They couldn't. No. These were very active souls, courageous and bright. The 2 cipher, we will remember, is passive only on its surface. Its subsurface 1 energy in the form of the 11 cipher gives it great action, direction and accomplishment, as is visible in the charts of these great pioneers.

Moon Flight

Aside from the ratification of the 19th Amendment establishing the female solidly within the political framework of American life, no other event of the Twentieth Century was more important in heralding the coming of the Age of the Female than that of landing a man on the moon and returning him safely to earth.

The Age of the Female: A Thousand Years of Yin

Certainly no other event in the history of recorded mankind has ever come close to being as profound and powerful.

During the entire existence of the human race on this planet, the moon hovered in the skies of earth like a magical, sparkling, crystal ball on a pedestal. She was separate from earth, glistening in the night-time sky like an exquisite pearl of renowned beauty, the object of poetry, prose and praise - distant, mysterious, unknown and . . . unreachable. Unreachable, that is, until the flight of Apollo 11.

America and the Soviet Union were competitors for the prize jewel of the moon. They raced. They sacrificed. They sparred. The fight was good for earth, for the outcome was that humankind began moving away from its own isolation as a heavenly body and into the realm of 'others' by finally setting a human foot on another celestial body, the moon. Man had now ventured off his own world (1) to contact, explore and interact with other worlds (2). Profound. Profound. Profound.

On 16 July 1969, the Apollo 11 spacecraft, manned by astronauts Neil A. Armstrong, Edwin E. Aldrin Jr. and Michael Collins, lifted off from Kennedy Space Center, Florida, planet Earth, in search of doing what no other human beings had ever done . . . set foot on the moon. The Lunar Module, inhabited by Armstrong and Aldrin, landed safely on the moon's surface on 20 July 1969 (a 2 calendar day). Collins stayed in the main spacecraft. A few hours later, Neil Armstrong, commander of the Apollo 11 mission, descended the ladder of their landing craft, placed his foot on the moon's surface and uttered the unforgettable and now historic phrase: *That's one small step for man; one giant leap for mankind.* Aldrin then joined him on the lunar surface to execute their assigned duties, which lasted for approximately twenty-one hours. They departed the moon's surface on 21 July and landed back on Earth in the Pacific Ocean on 24 July 1969. History, prodigiously profound history, had been made.

And this is why it is more profound than one might think. The rapidly approaching 2nd Millennium radiated the energy of and pulsated to the rhythm of not just the female but *others*. The moon has always been idealized by man in his literature as a feminine body, and it was definitely another, i.e., an *other*, planetary body as well. By man stepping onto the moon, earth man not only validated the oncoming reality of the 2nd Millennium, he unequivocally expanded his consciousness into the realm of *others*. Earthman was, actually and symbolically, moving away from the world of the 1 and into the world of the 2.

There's more. Apollo 11, with its 11 cipher, unmistakably and clearly exudes the symbol of the 2 energy (11 in its transition binary form). The Lunar Module landed on the 20th day of July, was explored by 2 men (astronauts Armstrong and Aldrin) and returned

The Age of the Female: A Thousand Years of Yin

safely to earth on 24 July 1969 – a 38/11/2 universal day within the Twentieth Century!

Furthermore, the major role in life (the PE cipher) of Neil Alden Armstrong, born 5 August 1930 (Armstrong), the first human being ever to set foot on the moon, was an 11/2 vibration! He also had an 11/2 Material Nature, a 2 Grand Challenge, an 11/2 2nd Epoch PE and an 11/2 Crown Challenge PE.

'Buzz' Aldrin, whose birth name was Edwin Eugene Aldrin, Jr., born on 20 January 1930 (Aldrin), had a 2 1st Epoch, 11/2 1st Epoch PE, 2 Grand Challenge, 2 Grand Challenge PE, 2 Crown Challenge and an 11/2 Crown Challenge PE. In stark contrast, Michael Collins, the astronaut circling in the Lunar Module while Armstrong and Aldrin walked on the moon, had no 2s in his chart! Pretty interesting, isn't it? The first two human beings to ever set foot on another celestial sphere, itself ruled by the number 2, both had 2 energy overflowing in their numerology charts while their flight comrade circling above the moon's surface and who never set foot on the moon at that time, had no 2s in his chart. Food for thought. Coincidence?

Still more. The logo of the 30th Anniversary of the Apollo 11 mission to the moon is below. Carefully notice its design. The moon and the number 11 are the logo's two most prominent features! Without question, the 2 Tidal Wave of the 2nd Millennium was relentlessly approaching during the Twentieth Century and making

King

itself known, not just in ciphers, but in symbols and signs as well.

Casual Note: when the two 'Ls' are extracted from the word Apollo, the remaining letters are: a - p - o - o. Add them up. The result . . . you guessed it, a 20/2! In multiple ways, mysterious ways, secret ways, divine ways, the vibrations of destiny make themselves known, and, to be sure, the destiny of Apollo 11, of taking the gargantuan step of taking a man out of his own world (1) and depositing him onto and into the fabric and surface of another world (2), almost leaves one speechless, breathless and . . . wondering.

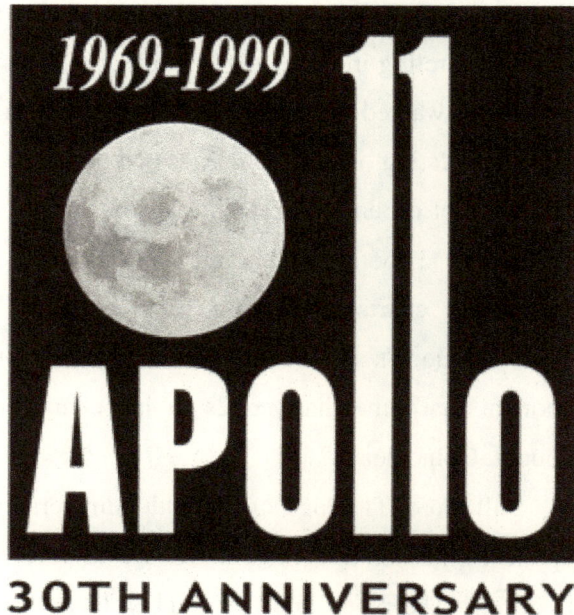

1969-1999 11
APOLLO
3OTH ANNIVERSARY

Picture courtesy of NASA

(Figure 1)

The Age of the Female: A Thousand Years of Yin

Pioneer 10

In keeping with the Twentieth Century's cosmic agenda of exploring other worlds, the marquee space headliner was Pioneer 10. Launched on 2 March 1972, this deep-space probe was the first to obtain close-up images of Jupiter, moving farther into the great void, exiting our solar system and moving beyond the Asteroid belt. It continued its lonely DSN (Deep Space Network) mission until its final feint signal was received by NASA on 23 January 2003, a time when Pioneer 10 had traveled a staggering 7.6 billion miles from earth in its 30 year lifespan.

From its launch date of 2 March 1972 (2 calendar day) until the receipt of its final signal by NASA on 23 January 2003 (11 Universal day [2 + 3 + 1 + 2 + 3 = 11/2]), Pioneer 10 contributed a vast amount of scientific data regarding the outer regions of our solar system. As an interstellar probe, Pioneer 10 was a star. However, as all stars eventually fade, so did the power source of Pioneer 10, and NASA engineers finally said good-bye to this stellar scout in February of 2003, allowing it to continue its voyage as a ghost ship into the unknown darkness of space. Her heading, the red star Aldebaran, which forms the eye of Taurus the Bull, which resides some sixty-eight light years from earth. The time it will take Pioneer 10 to reach Aldebaran is two million years (Pioneer)! And just in case it encounters other intelligent life, it is equipped with a plate picturing the nude forms

King

of a man (right arm elevated in a waving position) and woman; the outline of the probe, some mathematical ciphers and the location of our earth in relation to the center of our galaxy, the Milky Way (Pioneer Plaque).

The numerology of Pioneer 10 is as perfect as any could be. The 10, of course, reduces to a 1, the vibration of the pioneer and explorer. Additionally, the full Expression of Pioneer 10 is a 47/11/2 – the perfect pioneer (1) exploring the interstellar region of other worlds (2).

P	I	O	N	E	E	R	10			
7	9	6	5	5	5	9	1	= 47	>	11 > 2

The Computer

The significance of the computer in today's world needs no fanfare or explanation as to its unparalleled importance in our lives. Without computers, life as we know it would certainly be painfully and exasperatingly different. Everything, it seems, is computer-related. The computer and its global super-structure in the form of the World Wide Web have literally revolutionized the way the world wags, and it has single-handedly connected people in ways previously thought unimaginable. There is virtually no corner of the earth where the web's fibers have not been spun. Bringing 'others' in contact with 'others,' it is a veritable, visible and concrete manifestation of 2 energy.

The Age of the Female: A Thousand Years of Yin

One of the primary benefits of the internet is the free flow of information. Yet, such unrestricted flow is also one of man's greatest curses, for there exists the reality, which is steadily emerging, of people being involved too deeply and easily in the personal lives of others. Such involvement is not only intrusive but dangerous because it cuts at the very root of personal freedom and privacy. Without question, this will be one of the major ethical issues with which the world has to contend during this age if it desires to create balance, harmony and peace among its inhabitants.

The foregoing examples of the 11/2 energy as it applied itself to the technical aspects of the Twentieth Century (thus heralding the oncoming 2nd Millennium), are not the only instances of numerical expression needing attention. There's much more. We'll now leave technology, flight, space and the women's suffrage movement of the 1900s and move deeper into other 11/2 symbol, cipher and sign scenarios.

The Age of the Female: A Thousand Years of Yin

CHAPTER SIX

APPROACHING SIGNS II

The Yin
advances as the
coming Morrow moves in sight,
ever closer to her throne of light.
The tension of transition brings contention:
black and white, cast and clan, assassination;
walls fall, towers rise, massacres fill our eyes with tears;
all by design to redefine the substance of approaching
years.

The prophetic symbols, ciphers and signs of the Twentieth Century did not simply lend themselves to technological advancements and the suffrage movement. The field of human interaction was besieged with tensions of contention. Two world wars; civil rights movements between blacks and whites in America; cast and clan contrasts in India; clashes between the two super powers of the United States of America and the Union of Soviet Socialist Republics, assassinations of beloved world leaders, the rise and fall

King

of the Berlin Wall, the elevation of multiple sets of twin towers, the tragic deaths of heroes and heroines and the emergence of mass massacres filtering down from the ugliness of world war to the hallowed halls of education all pierced the human heart, mind and spirit with their poignant prongs of pain, progress and profundity.

What is extraordinary with the events and people mentioned in this chapter, as well as the previous chapter, is their combined association with the number Two. Such an amalgam of numeric connections can't be happenstance and, therefore, the science of numerology cannot also be happenstance. The language of numbers is, indeed, a secret divine code of an ordered universe.

THE EVENTS

World War

The population explosion of the Twentieth Century resulted, in part, in two global conflicts: World War I and World War II. World War I, supposedly the "the War to end all Wars," (how wonderful would it have been so) had been considered up to that time to be the one event having the greatest social and political impact in the annals of human history. Estimates are that more than sixty-one and a half million soldiers from all nations took part in the conflict. As the world began to shrink with the population explosion, its conflicts began to explode into larger wars encompassing the realm of many 'others' as represented by the 2 energy and its inherent negative quality of conflict, contention and competition.

Interestingly, the Armistice for World War 1 occurred during the 11th hour of the 11th day of the 11th month of 1918 (11 November 1918). Eleven/two, eleven/two, eleven/two (11/2 - 11/2 - 11/2)! One year later on 11 November (11-11) 1919, President Wilson of the United States proclaimed 11 November as Armistice Day, (Veterans Day) in commemoration of the war (Johnson).

World War II, with its Two energy unmistakably indicated in the Eleven structure of the Roman Numeral 11, ended on 2 September 1945, with the formal surrender of the Japanese aboard the U.S. battleship *Missouri* in Tokyo Bay (Grolier). The date of 2 September 1945 has the identical simple day/month numerical configuration as 11 September 2001 (2-9), the infamous World Trade Center tragedy now known universally as 911. Hauntingly, this gives World War 1, World War II, Veterans Day and 911 a 2 day of birth! All this in the Twentieth (2) Century. A 2 coincidence?

Event	Date	Simple
WW I - Armistice	11 Nov. 1918	2 Nov.
WW II - Surrender	02 Sept. 1945	2 Sept.
Veterans Day	11 Nov. 1919	2 Nov.
911 - Tragedy	11 Sept. 2001	2 Sept.

King

Another interesting fact about the global drama of World War II is that the core antagonist (villain), Adolf Hitler, was born on 20 April 1889 (Stokesey). Again, a 2 birth day giving him a 1st Epoch of 2, a 1st Challenge of 2 and a Grand (3rd/Core) Challenge of 2. Additionally, the name 'Adolf' is also a 2 in reduction, and the name 'Adolf Hitler' generates an 11/2 Expression.

The core protagonist (hero) or World War II was the English statesman, Winston Leonard Spencer Churchill who was born on 30 November 1874 and whose Expression is a 6. Churchill's numerology chart dons an 11/2 Second Epoch; a 2 Third Epoch; an 11/2 First Pinnacle PE and a 56/11/2 Crown Pinnacle (4th) PE. His Material Soul was also an 11/2! What does all this mean? Simply put, it was Winston Churchill's driving desire and destiny in his life to deal with the 11/2 energy – the energy of Adolf Hitler within the confines of World War II. This 11/2 energy is especially concentrated in Churchill's later years as indicated in his final Crown Pinnacle PE of 56/11/2 (the exact General Expression of Adolf Hitler!) and in his final (3rd) Epoch – the exact time period of his life when Hitler was attempting to take over Europe and in which he, Churchill, would have to engage and find ways to stop him. This Churchill did with his political genius, especially witnessed in his convincing the United States to enter the war (Schrepf).

The Age of the Female: A Thousand Years of Yin

These sets of numerical correspondences are quite remarkable. That Hitler should be an 11/2 (his Expression) and Winston Churchill's desire and Lifepath so heavily saturated with 11/2 energy indicates the synchronicity of life and its incomprehensible, numerical design. The propinquity of these numerical vibrations in their mutual charts is not coincidental. It is natural. It is spiritually scientific. In fact, were any person to know the numbers and numerical patterns of his life and those of the people around him, he would be astounded at the utter beauty, grandeur and perfection of it all because he would see the synchronization of the numbers between his own chart and those of the people and events to which he is intimately connected (for good or bad).

Numbers are people. People are numbers. Numbers also represent events, places, conditions. Everything in life is beautifully and perfectly integrated and connected . . . with numbers – the numerical God codes of all life.

There are no coincidences in the universe. All things have their define design – from people's destinies, to their relationships, to their personalities, roles in life, desires, conflicts, harmonies, achievements, successes and failures. We simply have to open our minds, place past preconceptions of that which we regard as real on hold and take a deep look beyond the veneer, beyond the surface, and into the depths and framework of that design.

King

Before man builds anything, he always formulates a blueprint first, a plan to follow. Would God work differently? Do we think man uses logic and science to construct something and God does not? Do we think man uses numbers in everything he does and God does not? Do we think that while the basic molecular structure of each element in the periodic table has order that the basic energetic/numerical structure of each of our lives is void of order? There is order to all things in this universe even though we may not be able to discern or understand it. Ignorance does not negate the reality of order anymore than ignorance negates the reality of gravity. Order exists. It is up to us to understand it.

When one studies numbers thoroughly enough, long enough and intensely enough and sees that all things, all people and all their associations, interrelationships and interactions have order and maintain a certain, defined destiny, which is generally (not specifically) knowable through numbers, one stands in absolute awe of whatever power there is that creates it all. It is far beyond the level of the intellect to comprehend. When viewing such immense perfection, integration, synchronization and orchestration, one simply shakes his head, closes his eyes and bows in unadulterated humility.

Civil Rights

On the 1st of December 1955 (20/2 calendar year) in Montgomery, Alabama, a forty-two year old African-American woman named Rosa Parks (born Rosa Louise McCauley on 4 February 1913) refused to relinquish her bus seat to a white passenger and move to a seat in the back of the bus, an area reserved for black Americans. Her courageous and defiant refusal ignited the civil rights movement in the United States, setting ablaze issues of freedom, fairness and justice for all people regardless of color. For this act of bravery, which started the wheels of social and civil revolution in America, Parks would eventually receive the United States Presidential Medal of Freedom in 1996 – the nation's highest civilian honor, and the Congressional Gold Medal in 1999 – awarded by Congress as its highest expression of national appreciation for distinguished achievements and contributions (Parks). However dauntless the defiant deed of Rosa Parks was on that December Thursday in 1955, a leader was needed to propel the civil rights movement forward. Enter Martin Luther King, Jr., born on 15 January 1929.

After Rosa Park's refusal to relinquish her seat on that most auspicious day of 1 December 1955, an organization called the Montgomery Improvement Association was formed to boycott buses in Montgomery, Alabama, in an effort to change the segregation laws. Martin Luther King Jr., a pastor in

126

Montgomery, Alabama, agreed to head that organization. The bus boycott lasted for 382 days. On 21 December 1956, the Supreme Court of the United States declared unconstitutional the laws requiring segregation on buses. Blacks and whites would ride buses as equals from then on.

Martin Luther King Jr. was elected president of the Southern Christian Leadership Conference in 1957, an organization formed to provide new leadership for the expanding civil rights movement. From that time until his assassination on 4 April 1968 eleven years later, King led the civil rights movement in America, traveling over six million miles, speaking over twenty-five hundred times and receiving the Nobel Peace Prize on 10 December 1964 at the age of thirty-five, the youngest man to ever receive this honor (Nobel Prize).

The civil rights movement of the mid-Twentieth Century in America was as reflective of the 2 energy as the women's suffrage movement was in the early 1900s. It is interesting that a female (Rosa Parks) was the ignition switch for the civil rights movement, but such is as it should be. Just as Elizabeth Cady Stanton had a plethora of 2 energy in her chart, so does Rosa Parks. Her Lifepath is a 20/2 (4 February 1913). Her Material Nature is an 11/2; her 2nd Epoch is a 2; her 1st Challenge is a 2 and both her Grand and Core Challenge PEs are 11/2s! So much of her life, therefore, revolved around the female Yin energy and the energy of others, in this case, equality for and among others, not just for women, but for all people of all races.

Martin Luther King, Jr. also had 2 energy is his chart, as one would expect by now. His 3rd Pinnacle was a 38/11/2 and his 2nd Challenge was a Two. The core theme of King's life was the establishment of justice, fairness and equality for all people, black or white.

Indian Independence

The struggle for civil and political rights during the Twentieth Century was not isolated to the United States alone. India also struggled for her independence from Great Britain. Her main advocate was Mohandas Karamchand Gandhi, born on 2 October 1869 (Gandhi). A lawyer by profession, Gandhi believed in equality and compassion for all living things. Non-violence and civil disobedience were his weapons of choice in India's struggle to become a sovereign nation, which it did on 15 August 1947, ending 200 years of British colonial rule (Indian Independence).

The 2 vibration in Gandhi's chart: 1st Epoch; 1st Challenge PE; Crown Pinnacle PE (4th Pinnacle), which ruled his life from age forty-six to his assassination on 30 January 1948. This was the same time span when he was most active in his work to gain civil rights and independence from Great Britain. Gandhi also had 11 in his 2nd House (on the #2 in his chart). Such a placement of the number 11 reflects dynamism and inspiration in the realm of others, relationships, peace, conflict, contention, balance and equilibrium.

Jackie Robinson

Today, professional sports leagues abound and are an admixture of black and white athletes. But it wasn't always so. There was a time during the first half of the Twentieth Century when only white athletes predominated the world of professional sports. There was no professional parity between black and white athletes. Enter Jackie Robinson.

Jack Roosevelt Robinson was born on 31 January 1919. Playing first base for the then Brooklyn Dodgers, Jackie Robinson broke through racial barriers by becoming the first African American to play professional major league baseball.

It was not an easy road. There was negative sentiment about Jackie entering the major leagues in the form of strike threats and petitions by managers and players (Robinson). But this was the emerging age of equality and equal rights, not just in politics but sports. Through the embodiment of Jackie Robinson, who went on to have a stellar professional career, major league baseball was desegregated. Black and white athletes would forevermore compete on the same teams, on the same playing fields, in the same leagues. Such professional equality in the world of baseball would set a trend for professional equality in other professional

The Age of the Female: A Thousand Years of Yin

sports. It was Jackie Robinson and his courage and character that led the way.

The 2s in Robinson's numbers: 11/2 Nature; 11/2 Grand Challenge; 11/2 Crown Challenge; a 2 Third Epoch; a 2 Second Epoch PE; a 2 Second Challenge PE; 22 in his 4th House and 33 in his 2nd House.

Black & White

It is sad but true that America has suffered racial tensions between her black and white brothers and sisters. Such tension must have some numerical correlation. And so it does. Interestingly, both of the words *black* and *white* are 11/2 vibrations in reduction and both have five letters. Therefore, it is no coincidence that a tug-o-war has existed between them. Hopefully, the higher ideals of the Two of peace, harmony and understanding will become manifest, relegating such tension to the history books.

B	L	A	C	K				
2	3	1	3	2	=	11	=	2

W	H	I	T	E						
5	8	9	2	5	=	29	=	11	=	2

King

130

The Kennedy Assassination

John Fitzgerald Kennedy (born: 29 May 1917) was the thirty-fifth President of the United States. A Democrat and Roman Catholic, Kennedy was the youngest man ever elected to the Presidency (1960 at age 43) and the youngest president to die in office, assassinated on 22 November 1963 (age 46) as his motorcade drove through Dealey Plaza, Dallas, Texas (JFK).

Assassinations have occurred throughout history and certainly JFK's assassination was not unusual for a global, national or American political figure. Although Kennedy's assassination has been shrouded in a cloud of mystery and conspiracy, it also had a profound impact on America and the world. There are probably many reasons for this, but one of them most certainly was exposure. JFK's murder by assassin was the first tragedy of its kind where the masses were connected visually by television, an event connecting the world of *others* like no other before it.

For those who witnessed that event live, who sat in front of the television the whole weekend from Friday to Monday – shocked, stunned, stultified and teary-eyed – it was incomprehensible and surreal. JFK was a young, handsome, charismatic, preeminently popular president whose wife, Jackie (born Jacqueline Lee Bouvier, 28 July 1929), was the quintessential epitome of a First Lady. She exuded grace, charm, intelligence, culture, courage, loveliness. JFK and Jackie were like the king and queen of America. They were both loved and greatly admired. It was like Camelot of King Arthur's Court and has been referred to as such by the press. Therefore, JFK's assassination wasn't just another presidential murder. It was the assassination of a dream. How could such an event happen in America? How could it happen to such a 'royal' family? Ideally, things so heinous weren't supposed to happen in Camelot.

With the killing of JFK, innocence died in America. Camelot was a fairy tale, not a reality, and when reality hit home in the hearts of Americans, there was a mental, emotional and spiritual shift like no other. And to see it happening . . . live before one's very eyes, before the magnetized, electrified, crying eyes of America, was almost beyond comprehension. Grown men cried in the streets, women wept, masses mourned miserably, heartbroken. It was the most visually griping and ripping moment in American history up until that time, an American tragedy whose scope was beyond the scope of understanding unless you were there. Approximately ninety-five percent of Americans were glued to television and radio during those horrendous four days from his assassination on Friday, 22 November, to his funeral on Monday, 25 November 1963. The average adult was reported to have watched the television for an average of eight hours per day during the event (JFK Assassination).

King

President Kennedy's murder brought into clear view what the evil and ugliness of *others* could do. Such a deed was not only unthinkable but unimaginable in those times. Thus, there was created a separation, a disconnection between dreams and reality. Good and evil existed together in one whole. From that tragic motorcade in which JFK was shot, to Jackie seen crawling on the trunk of the limousine in her pink attire in an apparent attempt to escape or help, to the on-camera killing of Lee Harvey Oswald (the ostensible lone gunman) by Jack Ruby as Oswald was being transported from a Dallas jail, to the riderless horse following JFK's coffin (Black Jack), to the multitude of mourners waiting in line outside the United States Capitol to see the body of JFK lying in state in the rotunda, to viewing Jackie Kennedy holding the hands of her children, then kneeling and kissing her husband's coffin draped with the Stars and Strips, to seeing little John John Kennedy saluting his father's memory, to the lighting of the eternal flame at JFK's grave site in Arlington National Cemetery, and listening to bullets crackling during the ensuing twenty-one gun honor guard salute – it was all so surreal . . . unreal, but nonetheless, sobbingly and soberingly very real.

To most of America at that time, JFK was a hero; his wife, not just a First Lady, but a queen. His assassination during the intense time of the Cold War between the two superpowers of the USA and the USSR was as heart-wrenching an American tragedy as there could ever be.

The 2 energy in the chart of John Fitzgerald Kennedy: 38/11/2 Soul Urge; 29/11/2 1st Epoch; 11/2 Grand Challenge; 11/2 Crown Challenge; 47/11/2 Crown Pinnacle; 65/11/2 Grand Pinnacle PE.

Furthermore, Kennedy was assassinated on 22 November 1963. This makes the 1st Challenge of this day an 11/2 (22 minus 11 = 11) denoting the treachery and deceit of others! Of note is that the universal day's corresponding 1st Pinnacle is a 33 (22 plus 11 = 33). 33 is the General Expression of the name *Kennedy*.

K	E	N	N	E	D	Y		
2	5	5	5	5	4	7	=	33

The Presidential Inaugural Address of JFK to the nation is a powerful piece of prose and numerological expression. This speech was delivered on 20 January 1961, a 38/11/2 Specific Expression Universal day (20 + 1 + 1961 = 38/11/2) as well as a 2 calendar day (20th of the month).

Jackie Kennedy, Queen of Camelot, is also not without an abundance of 11/2 energy in her chart: 11/2 Lifepath; 11/2 Soul Urge; 11/2 Nature; 11/2 2nd Epoch PE; 11/2 Grand Challenge PE; 11/2 Crown Challenge PE; 11 in her 2nd House; 22 in her 4th House.

1960 Counter-Culture

Other than giving us the assassination of JFK, the 1960s witnessed an enormous change in society and its mores and morals. These were the times of the Vietnam War, internal social conflict and a counter-culture movement whose core was comprised of hippies, psychedelic colors, recreational drugs, free sex, long hair on men (then unthinkable), peasant-like clothing and genuine anti-social behavior. It established a trend, many aspects of which are still with us today.

This decade of the Twentieth Century resonated with the vibration of the 2 energy of others and the clashing of individual ideals, philosophies and life styles of the counter-culture with those traditional American values held to be inviolate. It was a time of emotion where reason seemed to be taking a back seat to the popular counter-culture cry, "If it feels good, do it." Thus, the cosmic stage of earth was seeing the principal of reason, ruled by the number 1, giving way to the principal of emotion, ruled by the 2. The upheaval of the Millennia Shift rolled on.

Title IX

One of the important shackle-breaking events of the 20th Century giving women wings of flight was the passage of Title IX to the Constitution of the United States, signed into law on 23 June 1972, by President Richard Nixon. This landmark legislation banned sex discrimination in education for athletics and academics, discrimination which had been being practiced widely throughout the educational institutions of America prior to 1972, discrimination which held women back from gaining the degrees needed to compete in the workplace. But because the female energy of the 2nd Millennium was fast approaching, woman had to rise. She needed open doors for her energy to expand and express itself to the world. Title IX opened that door. It reads:

> No person in the United States shall, on the basis of sex, be excluded from participation in, be denied the benefits of, or be subject to discrimination under any educational programs or activity receiving federal financial assistance (Preamble to Title IX of the Education Amendments of 1972.)

To quote the U.S. Department of Education:

> Substantial progress has been made, for example, in overcoming the education gap that existed between men and women in completing four years of college. In 1971, 18 percent of female high school graduates were completing at least four years of college compared to 26 percent of their male peers. Today, that education gap no longer exists. Women now make up the majority of students

King

in America's colleges and universities in addition to making up the majority of those receiving master's degrees. Women are also entering business and law schools in record numbers. Indeed, the United States stands alone and is a world leader in opening the doors of higher education to women." (Title IX).

Quoting from the University of Iowa Gender Equity in Sports project:

Athletics has created the most controversy regarding Title IX, but its gains in education and academics are notable. Before Title IX, many schools saw no problem in refusing to admit women or having strict limits. Some statistics highlighting the advancements follow:

- In 1994, women received 38% of medical degrees, compared with 9% in 1972.
- In 1994, women earned 43% of law degrees, compared with 7% in 1972.
- In 1994, 44% of all doctoral degrees to U.S. citizens went to women, up from 25% in 1977 (Iowa).

The Age of the Female: A Thousand Years of Yin

Fall of the Berlin Wall

The number 2 represents division and the separation of singular 1s as reflected in the number 11. As we've discussed, the 11 can be two 1s walking along in harmonious agreement and accord, or it can represent two 1s moving in opposite directions, thus creating a tug-o-war, or the two 1s can be butting heads and clashing as they face off and fight. The later two create tensions, confliction and inharmonies. The greater the disparity between ideologies, the deeper the divide.

The Berlin Wall was a perfect example of this division represented by the 11/2 energy. After World War II, defeated Germany was divided into four occupation zones controlled by the United States, the Soviet Union, Great Britain and France. Berlin, approximately 110 miles from the western zone, was stranded in the midst of the Soviet Zone, but it also had four sectors occupied by the same four countries. All was fine for a while, but when the Cold War heated up and inhabitants from Communist and Soviet controlled East Berlin began to seek greater opportunity in West Berlin and possible escape to the free world, the Soviets erected a barrier, the Berlin Wall, to keep people confined to East Berlin and the Soviet block.

Known as the Concrete Curtain, the first vestiges of the Berlin Wall separating East and West Berlin were erected on 13 August 1961. Stronger and more elaborate means were used by the Soviets to solidify the wall during ensuing years, a wall which divided not just a city, but people, families and ideologies. As the Cold War came to a close and the Communist Soviet Union began to collapse, the Berlin Wall was reopened on 9 November 1989. Final destruction of this concrete divisor began on 13 June 1990 (Berlin Wall). The year 1990 reduces to a 19/10/1. Again the number 19, signifying concurrent beginnings and endings, appears in the numerological history of the 20th Century in a major way.

These three dates in the history of the Berlin Wall are amazingly profound because every significant date reduces to an 11/2 vibration!

The Berlin Wall: Significant Numbers

Initial Construction	$1 + 3 + 8 +$	
13 August 1961	$1 + 9 + 6 + 1 =$	29/11/2
Reopening	$9 + 1 + 1 +$	
9 November 1989	$1 + 9 + 8 + 9 =$	38/11/2
Initial Destruction	$1 + 3 + 6 +$	
13 June 1990	$1 + 9 + 9 + 0 =$	29/11/2

Additionally, the final destruction of the Berlin Wall began in its 29th year (29/11/2), just 8 weeks shy of its 29th birthday!

The Age of the Female: A Thousand Years of Yin

First Female U.S. Coin

Up until 1979, no factual female figure had ever appeared on a circulating United States coin. The honor of being the first woman on American coinage went to Susan B. Anthony, a pioneer of women's rights and a major player in the women's suffrage movement along with Elizabeth Cady Stanton (Anthony).

Like her suffragette partner, Elizabeth Cady Stanton, Susan B. Anthony's numerology chart (born Susan Brownell Anthony on 15 February 1820) is saturated with 2 energy, a fact which, by now, should not even bear the slightest resemblance of coincidence. Anthony's first name, Expression and Soul were both 11/2s. She also had 22 in her 2nd House, a Two 2nd Epoch, 11/2 Final Epoch and an 11/2 2nd Challenge PE. Anthony's whole life and destiny were immersed with female energy – from her deepest desires, to her personality, to the composite of who she was, to the very path of her life, through the middle years of her life, to its finale. The female energy was what crowned Susan B. Anthony and her destiny. How grateful should other women be that she never married but rather gave her life in sacrifice to promoting and pioneering the rights of women the world over, rewarded for her efforts by being the first woman whose face graced a U.S. coin.

1991

When we look at the cipher 1991 we are struck by two 9s set within the framework of two 1s. In other words, the number 11 with double 9s in the middle. Numerically, 1991 is a 2 year by addition and subsequent reduction. The result is a 20, a binary housing a 2 Pinnacle and a 2 Challenge.

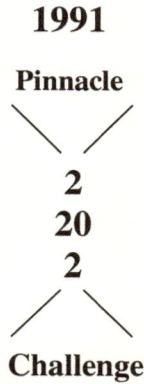

1991

Pinnacle

\ /

2

20

2

/ \

Challenge

The 1991 cipher focuses on action, beginnings, endings, power, global events and the 'many' encased in an energy field of others, division, contention, conflict – attributes of the 1, 2 and 9 ciphers. With this vibration we would expect a year where things would be starting and ending simultaneously and where there existed a good amount of tension and fire, both actually and metaphorically.

And so it was. 1991 was witness to two major global events: the fall of the Soviet Union in December, the once arch rival superpower of the United States, and

Desert Storm, the United Nations Coalition military operation spearheaded to remove Saddam Hussein from Kuwait and restore that country's sovereignty.

The fall of the Soviet Union may not have seemed like much of an event to those individuals born in the later part of the 1900s, but for those born in the first half of the Twentieth Century, it was a major event. The USSR and the United States came dangerously close to nuclear war during the Cuban missile crisis in October of 1962. The Soviets were sending ships to Cuba (its ally), ships supposedly carrying nuclear warheads. Not wanting to have enemy warheads so close to its borders, the United States objected and sent its own ships to intercept. The threat of war was so real that a large number of tactical and strategic aircraft of the United States Air Force had been deployed to Florida in the event of an attack. Tensions increased as the Soviet ships neared Cuba. Neither side was backing down. Finally, Nikita Kruschev, the leader of the Soviet Union, recalled his ships and war was averted. Therefore, to have the Soviet Union finally collapse in 1991 was a major world event. Here was a country whose sole goal in life was to bury the United States and establish Communism as the global ideology.

One date stands out in the fall of the USSR. There was a coup d'etat of the Soviet government by a group of hard-line Communists. On 19 August 1991 they announced on state television that President Mikhail

Gorbachev would no longer be able to govern. The coup, however, failed but it was not long after until the Soviet Union collapsed, and with it the threat of world Communism (USSR). The date 19 August 1991 is a 38/11/2 day! Looking familiar?

Desert Storm, of course, was another global issue but of greater interest. It was war, of sorts. Furthermore, it was televised. The whole world watched as coalition forces and Saddam Hussein's Republican Guard, et. al., went toe to toe in what Hussein claimed would be "the mother of all battles." The Liberation of Kuwait began with an air attack on 17 January 1991 at 2:38 A.M. – a 29/11/2 day. Iraq's army was destroyed in one of the most decisive and abbreviated wars in recorded history, hardly the mother of all battles. More accurately, it was the mother of all victories. On 3 March 1991, Iraqi leaders formally accepted cease fire terms (Desert Storm).

Thus, 1991 lived up to its numerological billing. The once mighty Soviet Union, superpower and advocate of global Communism, crumbled – an end which created a new world order without her as part of it. And . . . there was a new conflict with Saddam Hussein, and although there was an ending of sorts because he was expelled from Kuwait, he still withdrew to wreak havoc once again until his ultimate demise in 2003 with the liberation of Iraq by U.S. and British led forces, symbolized on April 9th with the toppling of a towering statue of the Iraqi president in the middle of Firdos Square in downtown Baghdad, Iraq. The calendar date of 9 April 2003 is a 9 Universal Day signifying endings $(4 + 9 + 2 + 3 = 18 > 1 + 8 = 9)$.

It's almost boring now, but the name Saddam Hussein is a 47/11/2!

S	A	D	D	A	M	H	U	S	S	E	I	N
1	1	4	4	1	4	8	3	1	1	5	9	5

$$= 47/11/2$$

Twin Towers

Another example of the 20th Century's portentous symbolism were two sets of stunning twin towers: the World Trade Center in New York and the Petronas Twin Towers, Kuala Lumpur, Malaysia. Both of these architectural wonders wonderfully, and quite distinctly, visually exhibit, not just the energy of the 2 but the energy of the 11!

Figure 2

(Photo courtesy of AdvancedElec.Com)

World Trade Center in New York: Pre-911

Figure 3

(Photo courtesy of the Petronas Corporation)

Petronas Twin Towers, Kuala Lumpur, Malaysia

Is it coincidental that these two sets of towers were constructed during the Twentieth Century, a century ruled by the 2 vibration, just cosmic milliseconds before the arrival of the 2nd Millennium? Is it coincidental that their appearance symbolically depicts the 11 cipher? Is it coincidental that, in form, they resemble the Apollo 11 Thirtieth Anniversary logo? They could have been constructed differently, not equal in size; they could also not have been sets of *twin* towers; yet, they were, and there wasn't just one set of twin towers in the world,

King

there were two! Is it also coincidental that part two of the New Line Cinema movie production, *The Lord of the Rings: The Two Towers*, was released in 2002, and itself focuses on the drama surrounding two towers? This may all seem far-fetched, but is it really? Why is it that the theme of twin towers became poignantly vogue during the 20th Century, just cosmic micro breaths before the arrival of the 2nd Millennium? Why?

911 -World Trade Center Tragedy

There have been two attacks on the World Trade Center in New York. The first was on 26 February 1993. A bomb blast in the underground garage complex displaced 6800 tons of material, created a hole 150 feet in diameter and 5 stories deep, filling the building with smoke and making it act like a 110 story smokestack; 6 people were killed and 1,000 people were injured (WTC First Attack).

The second and most destructive attack was on 11 September 2001, eight years later, in which both twin towers of the World Trade Center were totally destroyed, victims of terrorist hijacked airplane attacks. 911 is now, like Pearl Harbor (7 December 1942), an American historical event which will live in infamy. The numbers of this day are numerically significant.

There are far too many coincidences for the World Trade Center attack to be coincidental, the first being the date of the attack: 11 September 2001. The day itself (11 September) is obviously an 11/2 energy. The first Pinnacle and first Challenge are also Twos.

Pinnacle/Challenge Matrix
for 911

11

11   9

2

The 11th of September in any given year will always generate this particular alignment, so in itself this is not sufficient to generate any conclusive interest in that particular day. However, it was the first 11th of September in which the energies of the 2nd Millennium were activated by the 1 cipher (the calendar year 2001), a time period in which there would be new beginnings (1) in the realm of others (2).

The 11th of September 2001 was the 254th day of the year, an 11/2 in reduction. There were two twin towers in the numerical symbol of an 11 cipher which were destroyed, both of which contained 110 stories. The first of the two planes to impact was American Airlines flight 11 with 92 (11 in reduction) passengers on board, 11 of whom were flight personnel. Flight 77 had sixty-five passengers. Sixty-five is an 11/2 in reduction. Furthermore, the target city was New York, the 11th state added to the Union, which is composed of 11 letters (WTC-911). The alleged prime terrorist involved in the plot for this tragedy was Osama bin Laden whose Expression is a 47/11/2, exactly identical to that of Saddam Hussein.

O	S	A	M	A	B	I	N	L	A	D	E	N
6	1	1	4	1	2	9	5	3	1	4	5	5

$$= \quad 47/11/2$$

It has been suggested in some religious circles that the number 11 is diabolical. The number 11, as all numbers, has a positive and negative aspect to it. Deceit and the treachery of others is part of its negative aspect. Of this there is no doubt. However, the number 11 in its positive aspects is also a number of great inspiration and achievement. In addition to the cavalcade of positively noteworthy men and women already mentioned in this book, the word "Jesus" generates an 11/2 cipher. Diabolical?

911 may have been a tragic day in American history, but in its positive viewpoint it brought Americans together (2) in a way that has never been done before. The words "God Bless" were probably used

The Age of the Female: A Thousand Years of Yin

more times on 911 and in its aftermath than in the history of America, perhaps in the history of the world. Collectively, Americans did turn their attention Godward in a manner seldom seen in this country. They united and did so actively, dynamically, emotionally, courageously, historically as never before in the history of America. This was a good thing. Therefore, let us always look to the other side of the coin, any coin, before final assessments and conclusions are drawn. The Age of the Female is the Age of Balance, and if each of us strives for any modicum of peace, we must never forget that. Interestingly again, the phrase 'God Bless' is an 11/2 energy!

G	O	D	B	L	E	S	S
7	6	4	2	3	5	1	1

$$= 29/11/2$$

Columbine High School Massacre

It was 20 April 1999, the 110th anniversary of Adolf Hitler's birth (20 April 1889), a universal Lifepath day filled with 11/2 energy. On this day two teenage boys went on a shooting rampage at Columbine High School, Littleton, Colorado, killing 13 people and injuring 25 others. Unfortunately, this was not the first school shooting in American history, but it was the worst (Steel). Sadly, it may not be the last.

King

The 11/2 vibrations associated with the Columbine High School Massacre: First of all, it happened on a 2 day (the 20th of April 1999). The Grand Pinnacle of 20 April 1999 is a 56/11/2. Also occurring in this tragedy are an 11/2 1st Epoch PE, an 11/2 1st Challenge PE and a 65/11/2 Core Pinnacle PE – without a doubt, a day of extreme tension and conflict in the realm of others. Sadly, it was in the realm of children.

The intensity of the 11/2 energy filling the atmosphere of Columbine High on that tragic day was obvious. The hope, however, is that as a society we learn the lessons of spiritual nutrition, of tenderness, kindness, compassion, nobility, honor, honesty, integrity, virtue, ethics, goodness, fairness, respect and decency. It is these concepts which will balance the negative energy of the 11/2 cipher. If these values are ignored, we can expect to have more meaningless massacres like Columbine High, more tears, more sorrow, more suffering, more endless heartache and heartbreak. Children dying in cold blood at the hands of other children with cold, callous, cruel and indifferent hearts is unspeakably heinous. But the more germane question is, "What kind of message does such an event as the Columbine High massacre say about us as a culture?"

Heroines of the Shift

There were many great heroines whose lives impacted greatly on the Twentieth Century. Two such

The Age of the Female: A Thousand Years of Yin

women were Mother Teresa and Princess Diana of Wales, each passing from this life within the same week in August of 1997.

Mother Teresa

She was an Albanian immigrant, born Agnes-Gonxha Bojaxhiu on 27 August 1910. Known as the *Angel of Mercy* and *Saint of the Gutters*, Mother Teresa was arguably the greatest heroine of the Twentieth Century, epitomizing the nobility and goodness of the 2 energy. Traditionally trained as a Roman Catholic nun, she discarded her traditional habit, donned a sari – the traditional dress of Indian women, and sacrificed her life to give the light of life to others. She was selfless, supportive, pious, humble, deeply concerned and devoutly devoted to the well-being of the sick, giving dignity to the dying and love to lepers in the slums of Calcutta, India – a Hindu-dominated country (Mukherjee).

Mother Teresa bridged two worlds – those of Christianity and Hinduism. She was not simply another Christian proselytizer. She was a universal humanitarian in the mode of Albert Schweitzer and Gandhi. She was, indeed, a shining example for all people, a luminary of service to others. She once said: "In these twenty years of work among the people, I have come more and more to realize that it is being unwanted that is the worst disease that any human being can ever experience." Such

King

caring (2) and sensitivity (2) for others (2) were the basis of her greatness.

Mother Teresa, Leader of the Order of the Missionaries of Charity in India, was awarded the Nobel Prize for Peace in 1979. Quoting from her acceptance speech:

> I choose the poverty of our poor people. But I am grateful to receive (the Nobel) in the name of the hungry, the naked, the homeless, of the crippled, of the blind, of the lepers, of all those people who feel unwanted, unloved, uncared-for throughout society, people that have become a burden to the society and are shunned by everyone (Mother Teresa).

Additionally, Mother Teresa was awarded the United States Medal of Freedom in 1985. The *Angel of Mercy* and *Saint of the Gutters* died in Calcutta on 5 September 1997. The 2 energy in her 1 Lifepath chart: 11/2 Nature; 11/2 3rd Epoch; 38/11/2 Crown Pinnacle.

Princess Diana

Mirror, mirror, on the wall,
what can we learn
from the rise and fall
of a tear-laden princess
of the royal arts
who traded her crown
for a Queen of Hearts?
A tender child of tender years
whose need for love had turned to tears
in the wake of her parent's failing joy,
lamenting a girl; wishing a boy.
Such was the omen.
Frightful start – beginning life
with a wounded heart;
tender passions torn and worn;
unfaithful mother; bitter scorn;
endless nights of endless fears;
little brother's sea of tears –
crying, weeping, no mummy home;
big sister's cross – to walk alone.
The flower blossomed;
sweet youth in Spring
betrothed a prince
who would be king.
The marriage bargain –
fairy tale dream

King

for a tarnished crown

and a faithless ring.

Mirror, mirror, on the wall,

what can we learn

from the rise and fall

of a Princess hounded by a press,

void of manners and relentless;

stalking, never caring, forever blind

to the human need

for peace of mind;

for a little space; for a little breath? –

shameful, sinful, flashbulb death.

Mirror, mirror, in the sky,

faithful lovers question why;

young and lovely; future bright;

stolen dreams; fateful night;

why such a Princess, loved by all,

should reap the Whirlwind

and the Fall?

Mirror, mirror, in the night,

reflect a star whose beacon light

shone 'round the world

to hush a cry . . .

now shines forever

in a royal sky.

(King-Diana)

The Age of the Female: A Thousand Years of Yin

Princess Diana was born Diana Frances Spencer on 1 July 1961, dying tragically in a car crash on 31 August 1997 at the tender age of thirty-six, just 5 days before the death of Mother Teresa. Her death sent shock waves around the world. Not quite of the saintly quality as the Angel of Mercy and Saint of the Gutters, Princess Diana still possessed her own loving labels. She was heralded throughout the United Kingdom and the world as the *Queen of Hearts*, the *Princess of Love*, the *People's Princess* and *England's Rose*. And, like Mother Teresa, she had a special quality of love and compassion that endeared her to millions of people. She also had a divine destiny that far exceeded the ordinary scope of her extraordinary life.

During her life, Princess Diana was heralded as the most famous and most photographed woman in the history of the world. The span and spell of her embrace were almost beyond comprehension, as was the profound importance of her life. It is estimated that over half of the world's population, a total of some three billion people, watched her funeral. What person in the history of mankind has had such an audience in the aftermath of their death? No one. Such a degree of adoring adulation is unquestionably, even profoundly, remarkable. Why?

"Why" has to be asked because other than having been the wife of a potential English king and giving birth to two potential kings in the form of her sons William and Harry, what was her accomplishment in life? Think about it. In the thousand years of the British Empire, an empire upon which the sun never sat at one point in her stellar history, the Union Jack, the national flag of Great Britain, was never lowered to half mast, never . . . for anyone, including Winston Churchill – arguably the greatest statesman of the Twentieth Century, William Shakespeare – the greatest playwright of the English language, Sir Isaac Newton – the great English mathematician and scientist and on and on and on. England's history is overflowing with the achievement of distinguished souls who were not given the distinguished honor and recognition as that given to one Diana Frances Spencer for whom, for the first time in the thousand year history of the British Empire, the Union Jack, its national symbol, was lowered to half staff upon her passing. Furthermore, during Princess Diana's funeral procession, Queen Elizabeth graciously bowed her head as the coffin of the Queen of Hearts passed by, an act seldom, if ever, performed by English royalty. Again we ask, why?

The heart of the matter is to be found within the heart of the Queen of Hearts. Princess Diana was, for the most part, a common person like the rest of humanity. She had failings, faults, sins, shortcomings – just like we all do. But she was, for a time, English royalty. And . . . this is the key . . . her message in life was not one of monarchy and the distance and coolness normally reflected in the stiff upper lip mentally of British royalty, but rather, it was one of togetherness and compassion for others, the core wavelength of the Twentieth Century and the cresting tidal wave of the 2nd Millennium and its energy of the Yin which, at the time of her death knell, was ringing the door bell of the House of Earth.

Princess Diana was the essence of the 2 vibration. The timing of her life and the tragedy of her death made her an icon and a millennia bridge. The Age of the Male, the Age of Monarchy, the Age of the 1 – that thousand year period from the year 1000 to 1999, was exiting the world stage. Oncoming was the Age of the Female, ruled by the 2 energy manifested in the life energies of Diana Frances Spencer, a more or less common woman who lived an uncommon life, but whose message was about togetherness, sensitivity and others – hallmarks of the Age of the Female, the Age of Partnership, the Age of the 2. Thus, Princess Diana was in effect bridging the gap between the 1st and 2nd Millennia, a true Millennia Bridge.

Cosmically, the life and destiny of Princess Diana were perfectly placed; her life's mission perfectly executed. Had she died of old age, her message, more than likely, would have been missed. But because she died young and tragically, the arrows of loss, heartache, heartbreak and compassion hit squarely in the center of the heart of the common man and woman. Hence, Princess Diana became the Queen of Hearts, the People's

Princess. She was a divine instrument whose purpose was to usher in the consciousness of understanding, togetherness, compassion and others – positive aspects of the consciousness of the new millennium. And who was there more perfectly suited for such a role than a common girl radiating the energy of the 2 – the vibration of the oncoming 2nd Millennium, the Age of the Female – but living a life dominated by the outgoing 1 energy of the male and English monarchy? Thus, she bridged both the energy fields of the 1 and the 2. Simultaneously, the cosmic energies of the world were changing. The Millennia Shift was in full sway. Princess Diana was, for the common man, the bridge for that shift, and her role in life was to help usher in the ideals of the heart more than those of the crown.

As God speaks in symbols, there was a profound symbol in the wake of Diana's death which was openly showcased to the world. That symbol, as we have said, was the Union Jack flying at half mast, a symbol clearly depicting the approach of the Age of the Female and all of her attending qualities and characteristics.

In speaking with Jane Pauley of NBC during its coverage of Diana's funeral about the Union Jack flying at half-mast, Andrew Neil, Former Editor of the "Times of London" commented:

The Age of the Female: A Thousand Years of Yin

> If it had been left to the House of Windsor, you wouldn't be seeing that flag right now. The people put that flag there . . . Tradition has always been that the Queen's flag or the King's flag flies, never at half-mast, to represent the continuity of the nation . . . but protocol doesn't matter to these people . . . This is the People's Princess and these people are about to turn this into a 'peoples monarchy' (Neil).

When a flag flies at full mast, it represents union, solidarity, the 1. However, when a flag flies at half-mast, a universal acknowledgment of respect for the dead, the 1 of union is clearly bisected, separated into two parts. The flag flying at half-mast in honor of Princess Diana was, in effect, symbolically representing the ideals and principles of yin, which her life and death showcased. It was a sentient symbol with a clarion call: the age of the male, the age of the 1, the monarchy, had passed; it was now the age of the female, of others, of relationship, cooperation and compassion for all people regardless of status. The Age of the Female, the Age of Balance, the Age of the 2, not the 1, had arrived, and it did so through the tragic but glorious life of Diana Frances Spencer, Queen of Hearts and Princess of the People, who died during a fatal car crash in Paris, France, on 31 August 1997. Hauntingly, a 38/11/2 Universal day.

King

Full Mast/Half Mast
1 vs. 2: The Self & Others

There is interesting corroboration of the fact that Diana was, indeed, as Andrew Neil said, the People's Princess. During her funeral ceremony, her brother, Earl Spencer, gave a eulogy for his sister. The crowd within the abbey was quiet upon its conclusion. However, the crowd outside the abbey – common people who came to pay their respects – began to applaud for their Princess, and their resounding ovation sent a tidal wave of open celebration through the doors of the abbey and into the normally reserved emotional heart of those inside. Lord Jeffrey Archer, former British MP commented:

> I think really what was, probably, the most remarkable moment in what I would call my political career really, was that, after Earl Spencer had finished his speech, the applause started in the crowd outside; the people in the back of the abbey picked it up and joined in

and it moved through the abbey. . . It was a crowd-led reaction that the abbey picked up and joined in and that has been the case . . . All this week, the crowd, the people and the People's Princess were led by the people once again . . . None of us picked it up, that's the real point, until the crowd had let it. . .

Princess Diana's success and attraction was not because of her human achievements. It was because of her humanness. She was a normal person leading an abnormal life, and all the other persons who watched the drama of her life unfold before their very eyes got that. She was one of them, one of the common people at heart, and that's why she was the People's Princess and the Queen of Hearts. She was the queen of their hearts.

The Number 2 was powerfully placed in the chart of Princess Diana. The major role of her life was an 11/2 (PE). She also had an 11/2 Material Nature, a 2nd Epoch PE and an 11/2 Crown Challenge PE. Her royal marriage to Prince Charles was on 29 July 1981, making the 1st Epoch of their marriage an 11/2.

SUMMARY

"Numbers rule the universe" said Pythagoras. Indeed, they rule the universe in more ways than contemporary tradition may have suspected. To the ancients, however, the reality of numbers was fully

King

embraced. These two chapters of "Approaching Signs" have attempted to broach the divine design of life as it is reflected through the ancient science and art of numerology – the study of numbers. Some major examples correlating events of the Twentieth Century with numerical symbols, ciphers and signs have been presented. It is clearly extraordinary, if not mystifying, how so many of the major players and events of the 1900s revolve around and are centered in the numerical vibrations of the 11 and the 2 ciphers. Yet, the reality of the presence of these numbers in the lives, destinies and events of those mentioned is incontrovertible, leading one to entertain the veracity of a spiritual-cosmic order to all life.

This knowledge has been offered but seeks no argument. The sun is the center of our solar system; the earth revolves around the sun; the moon revolves around the earth; 1 plus 1 equals 2; tides rise, tides fall; seasons change; day turns to night; night turns to day; clocks tick away. What the human eye can perceive in the physical universe is limited to an extremely small part of the electromagnetic spectrum. What the mind can perceive is also limited by the range and scope of its ability. Mystics tell us there are regions far beyond the level of the mind, the reality of which can only be directly perceived by the soul. What, therefore, do numbers represent that we don't yet know? They certainly

The Age of the Female: A Thousand Years of Yin

represent something more than we currently know as is reflected by those facts offered here.

Do numbers define and describe life, destiny, reality? When viewing the facts, a sentient and scientific mind would seek to find the answers. Therefore, in final summation, let's review the number 11 and the number 2 as they appeared in the numerology charts of some of the major players and events of the Twentieth Century, those catalogued in the chapters 'Approaching Signs.'

TWENTIETH CENTURY
MAJOR PLAYERS & EVENTS

The Numbers 11 & 2

Elizabeth Cady Stanton   11/2 Specific Lifepath
Born 12 November 1815   Material Nature
Women's suffrage   Grand Challenge PE
          Crown Challenge PE

Suffrage   11/2 Expression

John Logie Baird   11/2 Crown Pinnacle
          Second Epoch PE and
          Second Challenge PE.

Wilbur Wright   11/2 Material Nature
Born: 16 April 1867   1st Pinnacle
          Crown Pinnacle
          1st Challenge PE

Orville Wright   11/2 Natural Soul
Born: 19 August 1871   1st Challenge
          2 Grand Challenge
          2 Crown Challenge

Kitty Hawk   11/2 Expression

The Age of the Female: A Thousand Years of Yin

1st Flight (Wrights)   11/2 1st Pinnacle
17 December 1903

Charles Augustus   2nd Epoch; 1st Challenge
Lindbergh   11/2 Grand Pinnacle
Born: 4 February 1902   11/2 Crown Pinnacle PE.

Spirit of St. Louis   11/2 Expression

Amelia Mary Earhart   11/2 Lifepath, 1st Pinnacle
Born: 24 July 1897   PE, Crown Pinnacle PE

Sputnik   11/2 Expression

Yuri Alexeyevich Gagarin   11/2 Lifepath, 2nd Pinnacle
Born: 9 March 1934   Grand Pinnacle PE
           2nd Challenge PE

Valentina Vladimirovna   11/2 Lifepath and
Tereshkova   Expression.
Born: 6 March 1937

Alan Bartlett Shepard Jr.   11/2 1st Pinnacle
Born: 18 November 1923   First Pinnacle PE
           2nd Epoch
           2nd Epoch PE

Sally Kristen Ride   11/2 Lifepath, Nature

Born: 26 May 1951   2nd Challenge

                                          1st Epoch PE

Neil Alden Armstrong   11/2 PE, Material Nature

Born: 5 August 1930   Grand Challenge

                                          2nd Epoch PE

                                          Crown Challenge PE

'Buzz' Aldrin   2 1st Epoch; 11/2

Edwin Eugene Aldrin, Jr.   1st Epoch PE

Born: 20 January 1930   2 Grand Challenge

                                          11/2 Grand Challenge PE

                                          2 Crown Challenge

                                          11/2 Crown Challenge PE

Apollo 11   11 as the identifying

                                          mission number

World War I - Armistice   11th hour - 11th day - 11th

11 November 1918   month of 1918

Veterans Day - Est.   11/2 1st Epoch

11 November 1919

World War II -   11/2 1st Pinnacle

Surrender   1st Epoch

2 September 1945

The Age of the Female: A Thousand Years of Yin

Adolf Hitler

Born: 20 April 1889

2 1st Epoch

2 1st Challenge

2 Grand Challenge

Adolf is a 2

Adolf Hitler a 56/11/2

Winston Leonard
Spencer Churchill

Born: 30 November 1874

11/2 Material Soul

2 2nd Epoch

2 3rd Epoch

11/2 1st Pinnacle PE

56/11/2 Crown Pinnacle PE

911

11 September 2001

11/2 1st Epoch

1st Pinnacle

2 1st Challenge

11/2 Expression

Rosa Parks

Rosa Louise McCauley

4 February 1913

2 Lifepath; 11/2 Material

Nature

2 2nd Epoch

2 1st Challenge

11/2 Grand Challenge PE

11/2 Crown Challenge PE

Martin Luther King, Jr.

Born: 15 January 1929

38/11/2 Grand Pinnacle

 2 2nd Challenge

Black

11/2 Expression

King

White	11/2 Expression
Mohandas Karamchand Gandhi Born: 2 October 1869	2 1st Epoch; 11/2 1st Challenge PE Crown Pinnacle PE
Jackie Robinson Jack Roosevelt Robinson 31 January 1919	11/2 Nature Grand Challenge Crown Challenge 2 3rd Epoch 2 2nd Epoch PE 2 2nd Challenge PE
John Fitzgerald Kennedy 29 May 1917	11/2 Soul, 11/2 1st Epoch Grand Challenge Crown Challenge Crown Pinnacle Grand Pinnacle PE
Jacqueline Lee Bouvier Born: 28 July 1929	11/2 Lifepath, Soul Nature 2nd Epoch PE Grand Challenge PE Crown Challenge PE
JFK's Inaugural Address 20 January 1961	11/2 Expression

The Age of the Female: A Thousand Years of Yin

JFK Assassination Date
22 November 1963

11/2 1st Challenge

Title IX
Born: 23 June 1972

11/2 1st Pinnacle

Berlin Wall
Construction: 13 August 1961
Opened: 9 Nov. 1989
Destruction: 13 June 1990

All of these days of construction, opening and destruction are 11/2 days! It was also destroyed in its 29th year (11/2), just 8 weeks shy of its 29th birthday

Susan B. Anthony
Susan Brownell Anthony
15 February 1820

11/2 First name, Expression and Soul. She also had 22 in her 2nd House, a Two 2nd Epoch, 11/2 Final Epoch and an 11/2 2nd Challenge PE.

Soviet coup d'etat fails-
heralds USSR end
19 August 1991

11/2 day

Desert Storm - begins
17 January 1991

11/2 day

170

Saddam Hussein	11/2 Expression
911	11/2 General Expression 2 First Pinnacle and First Challenge
Osama bin Laden	11/2 General Expression
God Bless	11/2 General Expression
Mother Teresa Agnes Gonxha Bojaxhiu 27 August 1910	11/2 Nature 3rd Epoch and Crown Pinnacle
Princess Diana of Wales Diana Frances Spencer 1 July 1961 Died: 31 August 1997	11/2 PE, Material Nature, 2nd Epoch PE Crown Challenge PE; married on the 29th of the month, a 29/11/2 day (29 July 1981). Day of death, 38/11/2 Universal Day.

CHAPTER SEVEN

CURRENT SIGNS

Intercurrent of what is past
and what is yet to come
is the all-surrounding Now –
the ever-present present
which presses the
exigencies of life.
Swirling currents of flood and flux
circulate and congregate
in whirlpools of living streams,
dreams which offer no escape
from the illusion of their reality
or the reality of their illusion.
Reined and chained we live and breathe.
Entombed and doomed in time and space
we taste the nectar and the poison of the times.
Advancing tides bequeath their mark;
receding waters cede their lines.
What is to come we gather from
the cavalcade of current signs.

King

FEMALE PROMINENCE

The first and most notable sign of this 2nd Millennium has been the rise of women, their placement and participation in a world previously dominated by men. In the year 1900 the male/female demographics were vastly different from those in the year 2000. Even though the one hundred year difference between these milestone marks seems large, it is in reality not much more than a cosmic blink. The female, although still expanding her influence, has solidified herself in practically every aspect of American society. As the millennium progresses, it is a safe bet she will continue to do so the world over. The earth is becoming extremely small, and the freedoms enjoyed by women in the free world will, with little doubt, be infused into other less free societies, if by no other process than social osmosis.

Yang dominated cultures will no longer be able to survive by ignoring the Yin because the simple fact is that the cosmic sun has set on the Yang day. The fires which energized him in the past have withered and waned. New fires, yin fires, fed by cosmic yin energy, will now radiate and serve as light and heat during this next millennium. For anyone to hang on to the old ways will spell disaster, the least dramatic effect of which will be a very cold existence. This is a new and different age, a new and different world demanding new and different paradigms, patterns, processes, procedures, parameters, points of view, strategies, schemes and means. What is past is past. The wise will adjust and move on. The unwise will perish or get dragged by the Yin bulldozer until they decide to get up and keep up.

In what part of the Western world today has woman not found a place of prominence? She has rooted herself in practically every field of endeavor. Government, law, politics, business, banking, financial planning, insurance, education, the military, medicine, health, athletics, aeronautics, law enforcement, public service, engineering, radio, television, science, sales, marketing, construction, communication, recreation, tourism, entertainment, advertising, tourism – you name it, she's in it. This was not the case fifty years ago in the 1950s and 1960s.

It is appropriate that the female be given her time on the great cosmic stage of earth. If God intended there to be one sexual gender, He would have created the hermaphroditic race, not the human race. The male had his moment. With the swinging of the cosmic pendulum, the female is being given her time. This is the natural order of things and as such should be well-received, if not embraced.

Therefore, a message to men: this is the time for women to have their place in the sun, just as you have had yours. Support them, allow them their moment. Give to them their just dues. Applaud them. Recognize them.

King

Be grateful for them. Neither disparage, ridicule or deprecate them. Edify them. Do what you do best, lead.

And women, your message: be gracious and also grateful. Avoid arrogance. Avoid vindictiveness. Enjoy your time in the spotlight. Excel, remembering the caveat of Jane Addams, Nobel Peace Laureate, 1931:

> I do not believe that women are better than men. We have not wrecked railroads, nor corrupted legislature, nor done many unholy things that men have done; but then we must remember that we have not had the chance (Addams).

That chance was soon to become reality. The curtain for the Age of the Female opened sixty-nine years later, right on schedule. By divine directive, woman took center stage when her image, in the form of the famous Lewis and Clark Shoshone Indian guide Sacagawea, was engraved on the first U.S. coin of the 2nd Millennium. The Sacagawea Golden Dollar debuted in January of the year 2000 (Sacagawea). The time for Yin had finally arrived. Her wait was over. The spotlight now shined on her.

And her role on the great life stage? Eerily, it's prophetically and profoundly encrypted on her golden dollar. Enwrapped by a blanket on her right shoulder, Sacagawea is carrying (and protecting) an infant. It is

The Age of the Female: A Thousand Years of Yin

not Atlas carrying the world on his shoulders (symbol of the Age of the Male) but a woman carrying a child on hers. Furthermore, there are two people on the coin, not one, as in previous coins. Even the Susan B. Anthony dollar was singular in image, symbolizing woman in ascendance but not in association with others. It was only the Sacagawea Golden Dollar that established the idea of others and partnership. Thus, the destiny of the female is unmistakably clear: for a thousand years She is to move in the world of *others* – sacrificing, supporting, guiding, protecting and nurturing in an atmosphere of cooperation and relationship.

OTHERS

Interconnectivity

As a part of the Yin solar system, the world of *others* is vast. Nonetheless, it is its own energy world and has many 'continents' within it, large masses of energy with their own characteristics, just as continents have their distinct attributes, topographies, climates and so forth. The 'continents' in the world of 'others' include, but are not limited to: relationships (general, commercial, romantic and familial), friendships, partnerships; support and help-oriented services; competitive athletics; diseases: human and machine; personal feelings; intuitive capabilities; business networking; television programming; racial, religious and ideological differences; spying, surveillance, data collection and other intrusive and invasive activities into private lives; terrorism; cloning and the search for and revelation of that which is hidden from view and resting beneath the surface of apparent reality.

Everywhere we look today, the energy and reality of 'others' saturates our life more so than ever before in human history. The trend will continue. After all, the 2nd Millennium has just begun. The themes and issues of the next thousand years are still being unveiled and revealed. As the population continues to increase, the pressure of living in a world filled with billions of other souls will become more pronounced and acute. Mankind will not spend the next millennium conquering lands and planting flags. He will spend it learning how to get along with his global neighbors, how to survive in a world of disparate ideologies and diverse cultures. Man's main issue now is people, not places. His activity will be interaction, not isolation.

Unlike times past, open seas and distant shores no more offer isolation from, and immunity to, the energies, ideologies, diseases and influences of others, be they positive or negative. Airplanes, computers, televisions, satellites, cell phones and other technologies have interwoven and intertwined us all in a web of immense global complexity. Now days, a country cannot sneeze without its repercussions being felt, not only on the other side of the world, but around the world. Economic interdependency is becoming more acute – in some ways distressing and afflictive; in other ways beneficial and acceptable, but in all ways binding, intertwining, interlacing, interconnecting and inextricable.

National autonomy is still alive, but the technologically reticulated nature of the global community is having a direct impact on the isolated sovereignty of world countries. Financially and culturally people all over the world are being brought together, sometimes through peaceful efforts and sometimes through conflict, but in spite of the means, the end is entanglement. Good? Bad? No judgments. It is what it is. The world is shrinking, its inhabitants weaving a web of intricate interaction and interdependency. Such is the way of the world of *others*, a world which, if it is to survive, must learn to manage its separate parts as well as the whole. The world social paradigm is now one of community, not individuality; synergism, not isolationism.

Diseases and Sexuality

In view of this interconnectivity, for example, take the harsh reality of disease. In times past, if a disease broke out in another part of the world, the rest of the world was relatively safe, insulated by geographical and oceanic boundaries. Enter the airplane, radio, television, computer and satellites during the 20th Century. All of these technologies contributed, not only to shrinking the world, but also in weaving a world wide web of interconnectivity. The airplane in particular made it possible to transfer people quickly and efficiently from one part of the world to another. It also made it possible to transfer their germs, viruses and diseases from place to place with the same efficiency.

AIDS (acquired immune deficiency syndrome) is one example of the global expansion of a disease. Caused by Human Immunodeficiency Virus or HIV and generally accepted to be a descendant of simian (monkey) immunodeficiency virus or SIV (HIV), the first proven AIDS death occurred in the Congo Republic of Africa in 1959, claiming deaths worldwide by 1978 and then widening its scope to become the worldwide crisis it is today. In 1997, for example, one study lists AIDS-related deaths at 6,400,000 and HIV-positive cases at 22,000,000(AIDS). Obviously, a true pandemic.

As was readily apparent during the 20th Century, and more than obvious during the opening scene of the 2nd Millennium, the open expression of sexuality has been on the rise. Sex seems to be saturating every area of the media – movies, magazines, newspapers, television, radio and the world wide web. More than ever, sex also seems to be absorbing people's lives, in some cases damaging them physically, emotionally, psychologically and financially. Sadly, sex, viz. a viz. AIDS and other sexually transmitted diseases, is destroying many of those lives.

The Age of the Female: A Thousand Years of Yin

SARS (severe acute respiratory syndrome) is another of the more notable, potentially lethal flu-like diseases which is making the inhabitants of earth incisively sensitive to the presence of others in our ever shrinking world. Beginning in November 2002, the disease surfaced in southern Guangdong province, China. It killed 34 people and infected 800 within a few months. It then made its way to Hong Kong, Vietnam, Singapore, Europe and North America (SARS) viz. a viz. passengers traveling by airplane.

SARS spread around the world in days. It also brought to mankind a spookish symbol of these congested, modern times – the macabre *mark of the mask*. On airplanes, in airports, in hospitals, on city streets and in an assortment of public places, people could be seen wearing protective masks across their mouths and noses in an effort to prevent contagion. Is this *mark of the mask* a sign of things and times to come during this millennium? There is now such a noticeable concentration and condensation of *others* in our world that people must be acutely aware of their own private worlds and the effect that other people's private worlds have on them. Living in isolation, it seems, is no longer a choice but a dream.

Influenza A (H5N1), also known as the Avian Flu, has garnered much attention in recent years. Although a bird virus, it does possess lethal potential. The concern is that if and when the virus learns to mutate in such a way that it is easily spread from human to human rather than from bird to human, the effects of a global pandemic could be devastating.

It is the sheer density of our world population which is partly responsible for the spread of the diseases we face. If 100 people were dispersed within a 100 square mile area, and if they were to have no contact, one person's disease or dis-ease would not affect another. However, place those same 100 people in an area of 100 square feet and the results would be dramatically different. In this sense, disease contagion can, therefore, be correlated to population condensation, a daunting fact of the new age.

The concerns of disease contamination are clearly reflected in the precautions taken to limit the transfer of diseases in the workplace. Wearing face masks to prevent the transference of SARS, as well as AIDS, has already been mentioned, but medical and dental personnel are also masking up. It is common today, for example, to have dentists wear, not only a face mask in their work, but also face shields and latex gloves. The medical profession is taking similar precautions to prevent the spread of disease in their environments, as are paramedics and other professions which serve the public. This trend began in the latter years of the 1900s but is becoming commonplace in this current era where the energy of others is more compact, more dangerous, more lethal. Having to wear face masks, shields, latex coverings and other devices to keep one safe from the diseases of others is an irrefutable sign of the menacing, hazardous and perilous times in which we live and breathe.

Diseases caused by viruses aren't restricted simply to living beings. Computer viruses have become a scourge and plague within the global internet community. These technologically generated diseases cause untold headaches to everyone, waste countless hours of time and cost billions of dollars to combat. Computer viruses can spread around the world in literally minutes and have. Probably no other thing reflects the interconnectivity of people throughout the world more than the computer and its global network, and there are few things in today's world more negative in a non-life threatening way than the insidious and nefarious contamination caused by PC germs.

Computer viruses are, indeed, one of the great plagues of the early 21st Century. Like any virus, they are systematically indiscriminate. They do not care who or what they contaminate. The good guys, the bad guys, viruses are non-selective. Everyone gets hit and is negatively affected. What is sad and troubling is that these are consciously and methodically created by people who have nothing better, more productive or positive to do with their lives than disturb, disrupt, interrupt, damage and inconvenience the lives of others.

King

The Internet

The World Wide Web is serving in the capacity of furthering the global intermingling of others. What newspaper of any major city on earth cannot be accessed through the web instantly to discover the news and events specific to its day and vicinity? Who is there who cannot potentially communicate with someone else in the world regardless of location in seconds? And language is hardly a barrier anymore. Software language translators make communicating with someone of a different 'tongue' quite possible. Video feeds make visual human interaction rich and real . . . in the blink of an eye. Mankind may not yet be on the same conscious wavelength, but the mechanisms and systems for him to be are being set in place.

The 'online' community of the world wide web is crossing all political, social, economical, geographical and religious lines, all without passports, restrictions and constrictions but also, and most unfortunately, often without conscience or compassion.

Borders of countries have been historically and traditionally defined as lines on a map, but where are the lines in cyberspace? Where are the borders and boundaries of the internet and its web? Where are the regulations? The controls? The respect for others and their views? The laws governing internet conscience?

Governments, for example, which have prohibited the free exchange of ideas, knowledge and information

The Age of the Female: A Thousand Years of Yin

can no longer keep their autonomous worlds segregated from the rest of the world. All one has to do is go online and he is immediately connected to the views, lifestyles, philosophies and ideologies of others around the world. Obviously, this poses austere predicaments for suppressive and limiting governmental regimes. Ideas can now travel from person to person, country to country, culture to culture at cyberspeed without sanction or censure.

Yet, sometimes when life moves too fast, people have difficulties adjusting. One of the main problems created by the web is that age-old ideals of certain societies, which have heretofore been held inviolate, are now being assaulted and threatened. Under this onslaught of clashing cultures, how could there not be tension? This is a perfect example of how the Eleven (11) energy creates anxiety and why we would all be well served to be patient and understanding. Changes take time, as do their adjustments.

Our earth is in the incipient stages of an historic mass merger which will probably be viewed in hindsight as the Great Global Convergence of the 21st Century. The wheels of worldwide integration are indeed turning; the connection is occurring at breakneck speed . . . as we breathe. Each one of us is an integral part of this unprecedented chronological confluence. We are living history, where 'living' is both a verb and the adjective of the noun phrase "living history." Without a doubt, these are exciting, stimulating, dramatic, uncertain, mercurial, transformative and revolutionary times!

However, there is a caveat. Although this technological progress has its merits, the World Wide Web is precisely that, a web. If we're not careful (personally and collectively), we will get caught in it, to our chagrin. Webs entrap. Echoes from the pensive pen of Sir Walter Scott ring frightfully clear: "Oh, what a tangled web we weave when first we practice to deceive" (from *Marmion/Lochinvar*).

Interpersonal Connection and the Media

Another example of how our world is shrinking while a web of our own making is expanding, is to consider television and its global programming. People in practically every country have indirect access to people in practically every other country viz. a viz. the boob tube. A myriad of television stations in a myriad of languages from a myriad of global communities constantly broadcast news, events, sports, game shows and movies to the rest of the world from their part of the world, all being mixed and mingled to create an environment involving others. A hundred years ago what happened on the other side of the world on a daily basis was virtually unknown and nobody really cared. Today, what is there that is not known or cannot be known, and because of the possibility of global conflict, who is there now who should not care?

The Age of the Female: A Thousand Years of Yin

Another interesting signpost of the Age of Others and the Female is the voluminous plethora of television shows focusing on the interpersonal aspects of people's lives. It's a common fact that women are more talkative than men and talk shows, for example, are the mainstay of not only television but radio programming.

'Reality TV' has also become a unique phenomenon. People seem to be highly interested in the intimate lives of others. Nothing seems to be sacred or off limits anymore. People want to know what goes on in people's private lives from survival expeditions, to family routines, romantic interludes, celebrity interactions, court dramas, adulterous affairs, match making and childhood births.

For those who are too young to remember, television wasn't always as personal or relationship driven as it is today. There was a time when western themes dominated the airways. Who can remember such popular cowboy shows as *Roy Rogers, The Lone Ranger, Hopalong Cassidy, Paladin, Wagon Train, Gene Autry, The Cisco Kid, Wild Bill Hickok, Kit Carson, Death Valley Days, Gunsmoke, Annie Oakley, Wyatt Earp, Cheyenne, Have Gun Will Travel, Maverick, Tombstone Territory, The Rifleman, Rawhide, Bonanza, Bat Masterson, Daniel Boone, the Wild, Wild West; Wanted Dead or Alive, The Rifleman, Big Valley, Black Bart, Branded* and *Laredo,* just to name a few. It's been documented that between the 1940s and the 1990s, over

145 made-for-TV westerns were broadcast. Some died quickly. Some survived. Some became traditions; others, classics (TV Westerns). That was then. Now is now. The winds and tides of time have brought a whole new set of tele-visions and messages to our visual world.

The current theme of interpersonal relationships dominating the airwaves has both positive and negative aspects. On the positive side, many people are speaking out about their life challenges, thus helping others to cope with similar, difficult issues they may be facing in their lives. Sensitive issues thought taboo before are being explored and expanding people's awareness. Feelings of honesty, sensitivity and compassion are being given open expression, which helps cut through the masks we all wear from time to time. Qualities of support, helpfulness, compassion and understanding are being engendered and promoted.

On the negative side of this 2 interpersonal energy reflected in television programming is the insensitivity, unkindness and callousness of some shows, their hosts, guests and audiences. Being rude, crude, coarse and crass is being depicted as acceptable, laudable and applaudable social behavior. Hurting the feelings of others seems to warrant badges of pride and virtue. Inconsiderate, thoughtless diatribes or denigrating commentaries directed toward others are manifesting like ugly, oozing, gangrenous boils. Where does this type of negativity originate? Why is it being promoted and applauded? Has our ability to be compassionate and caring withered to such an extent that we find comfort and entertainment in ridiculing, degrading, denigrating, abusing, misusing and hurting others and taking pleasure in it all? What are the messages of these messages?

Does not all this type of activity leave one to ponder the character composition of a society seemingly on the verge of being out of ethical control and in speedy descent? Qualities of honor, dignity, propriety, manners, kindness, compassion, edification and acceptable good humor seem to be being left behind in the race for ratings, laughs and personal pleasure, as some television shows pander to the most base and banal desires of the human mind. 'Civilized' humanity seems to be becoming more uncivilized by the day. Whatever happened to basic goodness, purity, virtue, grace and dignity? Is not much of today's television programming antithetical to the nobility of the human spirit, as well as being an unflattering commentary on the level of our human collective consciousness?

What does such ignobility say about the spiritual and psychological maturity of our civilization, the root word of which is *civil*? What does it say about the direction in which we're headed as a society? Are we becoming more concerned about taking our pleasure from the pain, suffering, anguish, ridicule and embarrassment of others, rather than from those actions which edify and purify the spirit and consciousness? Is our race becoming base?

If man is so high on the evolutionary ladder, why does he do things that other living beings would never think of doing? Just for starters, horses, dogs and cats don't behave in many of the negative ways many humans do. The later group on the whole exhibits behaviors which are in many ways noble, loyal, devoted, forgiving and non-ridiculing to other living beings. Yet, they are considered lower than man on the evolutionary ladder. Therefore, what does such behavior say about animals? What does man's behavior say about him? Supposedly, man has been given a superior mind and exalted status among all living beings, but many of his actions reside far below the level of animal behavior. To be sure, ridicule, denigration, degradation, humiliation and disrespect are not superior attributes and frankly demean man and warrant his embarrassment, which may be one of the reasons Napoleon said: "We must laugh at man to avoid crying for him." A few quotes from Confucius are also germane to this discussion:

> The man of virtue makes the difficulty to
> be overcome his first business and success
> only a subsequent consideration.

> The superior man understands what is right;
> the inferior man understands what will sell.

The Age of the Female: A Thousand Years of Yin

The superior man is distressed by the limitations of his ability; he is not distressed by the fact that men do not recognize the ability that he has (Confucius 1).

Without recognizing the ordinances of Heaven, it is impossible to be a superior man (Confucius 2).

Information Gathering

In our society today the amount of data collection is alarming. Information gathering is at an all-time high. Data banks in all areas of society are being filled with as much personal information as possible. What a professional security investigator today can obtain from available data banks would startle most people, if not frighten them. Yet, society seems to parade on, oblivious to and totally unconcerned with the personal profiling undermining individual privacy.

Just think of identity theft. Commonplace today? Of course. People's identities are constantly being stolen, their financial forts assaulted. Data banks are being robbed far too often of their precious contents – personal information. Such identity theft could not occur if there were not such a critical depository of individual data awaiting the sinister touch of some cyber thief lurking in the shadows with a PC and a keyboard.

A simple experiment: look around at how often you are asked for unnecessary personal information – at retail stores, shopping clubs, doctor and dental offices, insurance companies, online questionnaires, etc.? It seems everyone wants information, as much as they can get, although it may neither be legal nor ethically appropriate for people to ask for such information. Social security numbers are critical to keep private because they reside at the core of one's personal identity. Few people other than law enforcement officers have a right to such information, and it would be unwise to share it openly and willingly. Critical personal information should be regarded as sacrosanct and guarded appropriately. The deceit and treachery of identify theft, however, is most likely not going to go away. Nor is the accumulation of personal data. Therefore, people must be ever watchful over all of their valuable assets in this age, assets of both the financial and information varieties.

It is a truly sad and tragic state of affairs that the qualities of duplicity and deceit are running rampant in our society, so much so that many people do not recognize them or even deny, defend and accept them as appropriate to personal interaction, profitable business or acceptable living standards. Unfortunately, such characteristics are one aspect of the negative side of the

2 energy, and all of us will have to learn to deal with them and protect ourselves from them. While there are decent, ethical and upstanding people in the world, there are also those who are indecent, unethical and unprincipled. Wolves do cavort themselves in sheep's clothing, and therefore it is incumbent that greater discernment and discrimination be exercised in matters of personal safety, protection and concern.

Competitive Athletics

Of all of the manifestations of the 2 energy, none is more visible than competitive athletics, both on an amateur and professional basis. They dominate modern culture in a myriad of ways and are an extremely healthy way for people to express their basic oppositional energies. Yes, there are cases where athletic passions have gotten out of hand, and, yes, there are defensible arguments for not involving children too early in the competitive process, but the world will never be without competition or contention. It is the way of life in this duality-based creation. There is positive; there is negative. There is victory; there is defeat. There is one guy's claim to superiority and another guy's counterclaim. Thus, competition thrives. In this 2nd Millennium there will be no dearth of lines being drawn in the sand or gauntlets thrown down to force a challenge.

The 20th Century has seen the rise of competitive athletics, just as it has dramatically seen the rise of the number of people in the world. Once relegated pretty much to males, females didn't compete on a broad scale until the latter part of the century. The passage of Title IX in 1972 banning sex discrimination in federally funded educational institutions in academics, as well as athletics, obviously changed the playing field, at least for American women, opening opportunities for them to compete, opportunities previously denied them.

It's not just individuals and teams that are involved in competitive athletics but a sea of spectators as well. What major U.S. city doesn't have or has never had a professional athletic team or teams of some sort? How many major cities in the world have their sports formats and venues? How many millions of people and billions of dollars the world over are spent annually, directly and indirectly on competitive sports – professional, amateur, educational, recreational? There is no doubt the clashing of players and teams will continue to thrive. It is classic yin vs. yang.

The advantages of competition lie in the process of struggling to attain a certain mark of excellence. That excellence is usually signified as triumph over adversity or an adversary. Qualities of physical prowess, strength of will and mind, courage, confidence, concentration, coordination, dedication, determination, duty, discipline, devotion, responsibility, accountability, flexibility, cooperation, teamwork, sharing, grace under pressure, grace in victory, grace in defeat, character in general, humility and balance are all positive by-products of the competitive process. When it comes to competitive athletics it is not so much the trophies that are important, it is the things learned and experienced during the training that are important. Indeed, in the world of competitive athletics the process is the product.

When we think of competition, we normally think of competing with others. But in truth, the greatest competition is not with other selves but with our own selves. Life is a constant struggle, a struggle for survival, a struggle to stay balanced, whole, happy, harmonious, calm, focused, committed to a code of life and set of personal ethics which define who we are as human beings. Who is there who has not struggled? Rich or poor, beautiful or ugly, famous or infamous, fat or thin, male or female, adult or child – all struggle. Such is the nature of this world, a wrestling ground between right and wrong, light and dark, positive and negative, what we should do rather than what we could do. The pendulum keeps swaying back and forth, to and fro, and we are forever trying to manage its ever-turning tides. Hopefully, we compete with ourselves to better ourselves, to reach a pinnacle of excellence we haven't reached before, rather than competing simply to prove our superiority over others and/or their subjugation to us.

King

Because the number 2 rules opposition, division and contention, there will always be competition, especially during this age. Nature has established her own intrinsic tug-o-war paradigm and there is no way we can escape it unless we rise above it. That's unlikely in the main. The factual reality is that this is a competitive world. It's not going to change. The key, therefore, is to keep it constructive, not destructive; ethical, not unethical; honorable, not dishonorable; noble, not ignoble.

In consideration of the competitive arena, Leora Tanenbaum has authored a book entitled, "Catfight." Published by Seven Stories Press, Tanenbaum dissects the gender war waged among females, meticulously analyzing the destructiveness of women vs. women (a natural Age of the Female title). She asserts that catfights thrive because women have been conditioned to view other women as adversaries, not allies. She also addresses the issues of women being indirect in their conduct and doing things underneath the surface (Tanenbaum). Interesting. These issues which Tanenbaum discusses: competitiveness, adversaries, fighting, indirection and sub-surface action are all expressions and manifestations of the 2 energy. Will this trend with women being prone to catfights continue during The Age of the Female? Will women learn to be less competitive with each other or more cooperative? Most assuredly, time will tell.

The Age of the Female: A Thousand Years of Yin

Business Intuition - Networking

As we know, the number 2 possess a great deal of sub-surface energy as represented by its 11 transition root. One of the ways this sub-surface energy is manifested is through the faculty of intuition – knowing or sensing something without the use of rational processes. Women have always been known for their intuition as is corroborated by the phrase, "A woman's intuition." This is natural since the number 2 rules both women and intuition.

However, with the 2 energy now dominate in our world, many male corporate executives are relying on their intuition, not their reason, to make decisions and solve problems. Historically, men have not been known for their intuitive skills. After all, no one has ever even dreamed up the phrase, "A man's intuition."

In an article entitled, "How to Think With Your Gut," Thomas A. Stewart explores the concept of intuition in the business and combative environments of the present era. He states:

> People who make decisions for a living are coming to realize that in complex or chaotic situations – a battlefield, a trading floor, or today's brutally competitive business environment – intuition usually beats rational analysis. And as science looks closer, it is coming to see that intuition is not a gift but a

skill. And, like any skill, it's something you can learn.

Stewart explains in the article that within the realm of complexity, decisions usually come from the gut, not the mind, establishing the theory that instinct is better than rational analysis. He corroborates this theory with the story of Paul Van Riper, a retired Marine Corps Lieutenant General who experimented with rational versus intuitive thought. In his experiment, General Riper pitted his own Marines against stock traders on the floor of the New York Mercantile Exchange in 1995. Not surprisingly, the traders wiped out the Marines. The astonishing thing, however, was that when the stock traders and the Marines competed in war games a month later, the traders thrashed the Marines again, this time at their own game! The reason: the traders were simply better gut thinkers (Stewart).

In considering whether a rational or intuitive approach is better for real life decision making, Stewart surmises that the best approach lies somewhere between the two extremes. However, it is fascinating that in this Age of the Female, the faculty of intuition is gaining prominent recognition, not only in the business environment but also within the scope of the male decision-making process.

Another aspect of the 2 vibration, which began approximately in the later part of the 20th Century, is the

The Age of the Female: A Thousand Years of Yin

now-commonplace concept of networking, the process of action through inter-connection with others. Networking is pure 2 energy. It is a clear manifestation of partnership and relationship in action. In today's complex and fast-paced world, it is difficult to go it alone. One's success is now poignantly predicated on working with others in an atmosphere of harmonious and productive relationship, i.e., networking.

Yet another manifestation of the 2 energy within the business environment is the concept of the team player. How often in the last decade or so has a company referred to itself as "team this" or "team that." Being a part of the "team" is a prominent aspect of contemporary business enterprise. To be considered a lone wolf, a maverick or a loner of some sort is not in vogue, although it used to be. Now days, the concept of the team is taking precedence, and what is a team except a group of people, of others, working together in a coordinated capacity.

Sensitivities - Insensitivities - Courage

Another issue of this Age of Others is the concept of 'political correctness,' socially referred to as 'PC.' How closely are people guarded in their vocabulary these days? How sensitive or even hypersensitive have we become as a people, and what does this reflect on our personal completeness? Are we becoming too emotionally soft? Too incomplete? Too concerned about what others think about us, about their validation of us? How many "politically correct" statements are, frankly, silly? Are we, in fact, becoming too fragile? Or are we becoming too insensitive, cold, callous and apathetic? Arguably, in being overtly politically correct, have we not lost our perspective and sensibility, swinging too far to the opposite polarity and becoming, in fact, incorrect?

Semantic propriety certainly has its place in social situations. Hurting the feelings of another or others is inappropriate, but isn't having to be so guarded in the use of language that the common normal flow of personal relations is inhibited because someone's overly delicate sensitivities and feelings may get hurt going a little too far overboard? Somebody will always be hurt by whatever is said, and to have to worry about every little word and its ramifications borders on the absurd and ridiculous.

Whatever happened to emotional toughness? Where would the world be if those brave, courageous and daring souls who pioneered the formidable frontiers of earth took offense at every unkind, harsh and ridiculing word directed at them and thereby buckled under the weight of those words? Who would have ever pushed forward, pushing the frontier back and making way for the mass of humanity to follow? In the words of the famous American actress Bette Davis:

> There are new words now that excuse
> everybody. Give me the good old days of

The Age of the Female: A Thousand Years of Yin

heroes and villains, the people you can bravo
or hiss. There was a truth to them that all the
slick credulity of today cannot touch
(Brainyquote, Davis).

What ever happened to individuals believing in the
substance of the phrase, "Sticks and stones may break
my bones, but words will never hurt me?" It's getting to
a point in our society where that phrase is in perilous
danger of being altered to, "Sticks and stones may break
my bones and every little word will crush me." God
forbid that ever happens because it would be an
abominable shame, as well as a tragedy and travesty to
the glory of the indomitable human spirit.

Where would women be today if it were not for the
Susan B. Anthonys, Elizabeth Cady Stantons, Lucretia
Motts, Babe Didriksons, Amelia Earharts, Valentina
Tereshkovas, Eleanor Roosevelts, Margaret Thatchers,
Margaret Meads, Golda Meirs, Indira Gandhis, Billy
Jean Kings, Jean Driscolls, Janet Guthries, Wilma
Rudolphs, Julie Krones, Barbara Walters, Sandra Day
O'Connors and Oprah Winfreys of the world? These
were and are brave, valiant, courageous, tough and
daring women who pushed ahead in their chosen fields
in spite of public criticism, ridicule and censure. And
don't think they weren't getting the censure, the ridicule,
the unkind words, the gossip, the lies, the innuendoes,
the looks, the stares, the cold shoulders. These were not

King

weak females. Nor were they most definitely not sissies or cry babies. They were and are strong, tough, focused, determined women with a vision and the power to materialize that vision. If they had cried or whined or whimpered or complained every time someone directed a derogatory or untoward comment toward them, the women's movement would still be in the dark ages, lamenting that it's still a man's world. In fact, these were not simply great women, they were and are great souls with the type of emotional power and balance that did not betray their accomplishments, their sexuality, nor their humanity. Brava! Brava! Brava!

These examples have been just a few of the current signs of the times. Yet, there are also grave issues needing addressing. Let's take a look now at some of the concerns and dangers of our new age.

CHAPTER EIGHT

CONCERNS & DANGERS

The trip begins – just inches in
on a thousand mile road;
what lies ahead as travelers tread
the path is writ in code.

Sunny rays and shaky days
no doubt will take their turns,
aligning the path circuitous
with dangers and concerns.

To hide the head and never dread
the route of unknown seas,
denies the wise and insures cries
of trailing miseries.

The path ahead is marked by Two:
divisions, tensions, rivals, strangers;
intruding eyes, Orwellian skies
disguise concerns and dangers;
create concerns and dangers;
concerns and dangers;
dangers.

King

There is no trail without its tears . . . or fears. Great things may be accomplished by the end of the journey, but much is usually sacrificed along the way. To believe there can be attainment without struggle is to deny the obvious. To believe there can be beauty without ugliness is to misunderstand beauty. To believe that life is a bed of roses is to have never felt the rose's thorns. To be oblivious to the reality of concerns and dangers on the road ahead is not only unwise, it is potentially unhealthy, incarcerating and lethal.

THE LOSS OF YANG

With the changing of any guard there is always a restructuring of the status quo. Some things get left behind – some good, some bad. So it is with the Millennia Shift from Yang to Yin, from 1 to 2. Some elements of the last millennium are being left behind. Certainly there are characteristics of the 1 energy which are undesirable, and no one will have any love lost for losing them. The 1 energy can be overly aggressive, ego-centric, selfish, harsh, unreasonably unbending, distant, excessively solitary and demanding. But there are many positive qualities of the Yang as well which are critical to wholeness and well-being, and if lost or minimized would pose grave difficulties – individually and collectively.

The Age of the Female: A Thousand Years of Yin

Let it be said that the qualities of the 1 vibration will not be completely expunged from the face of the earth simply because the 2 energy is now dominant. Far be it. The keyword to note is 'dominant.' Whereas in the last thousand years the yang was dominant, it is now time for the yin to be highlighted in the main. Yang qualities will still be present, but to what extent? That is the question.

Like its symbol of the sun and its element of fire, the yang (ruled by the number 1) has many positive characteristics which not only create life, but allow for a high quality of that life. In fact, how could there be life without the sun and its life-giving light? How long would any living thing last without it? Ask any dinosaur. Furthermore, what would the quality of life be without fire? Ask any corpse who froze to death. Without 1 energy, which rules both light and fire, life would cease to exist. Some of the positive attributes of the 1 which are essential to life are independence, achievement, leadership, decisive action, reason, linear thought, directness, creativity, originality, strength, courage, will power, raw power, responsibility, accountability, confidence, concentration, separation, vision, union and divine Oneness.

The 1 vibration stands alone. Without it there would never have been nor will there ever be a pioneer to blaze new trails within the landscape of forbidden and formidable frontiers. The 1 is a leader who goes first and shows the way; whose knees never buckle in the face of fear or opposition; who stands up to his adversaries, looks them eye to eye and never backs down from those values and virtues ancient wisdom holds to be inviolate. The 1 also has the courage to stand separate from the crowd, lift its arm, motion it forward and boldly exclaim, "Follow me!" In essence, without the singular power of the 1 there could be no leaders, authority figures or rulers to give direction. Nothing would be unique, different or original because there would be no creative thought or action to generate it. Everything would simply be the same, look the same and act the same.

The 1 is the achiever who abhors mediocrity and is constantly directing his focus upward and onward to new and different horizons. Ones are rebels and loners, not mixers, team players or hand-holders. They are the solo players of the numeric spectrum and definitely walk to the beat of their own drum and will fall off their path if they do not. They must be their own person and make their own way in the world, and for them to deny their unique and singular individuality would be a tragedy.

Biologically, without the male – the physically manifest form of the 1, women could not conceive, directly or indirectly. Without the 1 there would be no sense of purpose. Most sadly of all, without the 1 there could be no understanding of God or divine life because the 1 represents Union, at-one-ment with the Almighty, and where there is no union (yoga) there is division and,

The Age of the Female: A Thousand Years of Yin

by definition, division is separation, not centralization. In effect, without the 1, man would be lost and forsaken.

Helen Keller was certainly one of the most courageous, creative, independent, strong willed and pro-active luminaries exemplary of the 1 vibration. The spirit of her 1 energy is captured when she says:

> I am only one, but still I am one. I cannot do everything, but still I can do something, and because I cannot do everything I will not refuse to do the something that I can do (Bella).

Not surprisingly, Keller's Expression was a One (1)

H E L E N A D A M S K E L L E R
8 5 3 5 5 1 4 1 4 1 2 5 3 3 5 9

$$= \quad 64 > 10 > 1$$

How sad would it be if the qualities of courage, vision, action, independence, responsibility and leadership as those expressed by Helen Keller were lost? Even though our earth is immersed in the Two energy, we must not be blind, nor leave behind the One. The best strategy is to embrace both energies, bringing them into a state of perfect equilibrium. Then one would have the best of both worlds.

King

2nd MILLENNIUM SLAVERY

Why this focus on the 1? Aren't we in the age of the 2? Precisely, and that's the great danger. One of the attributes of the Two is that it ties and binds. With the technological advancements of the modern age and a desire for an easy, comfortable life, the world is frighteningly close to being tied and bound by the manacles of computerized wizardry and the machinations of maniacal wizards. Minute by minute, hour by hour, day by day, inhabitants of earth are being incarcerated with the shackles of George Orwell's Big Brother.

With the advent of super computers and biochip technology, the people of the world stand precariously on the precipice of bioslavery, a condition of abject subjection where people's lives and minds, not so much their bodies, become incarcerated in an inextricable web of technological captivity.

In his poem *To Althea From Prison*, 17th Century, Oxford educated poet Richard Lovelace states:

> *Stone walls do not a prison make*
> *Nor iron bars a cage;*
> *Minds innocent and quiet take*
> *That for an hermitage.*

Lovelace is basically saying that even though one's body may be chained in prison, one's mind cannot be

The Age of the Female: A Thousand Years of Yin

chained, cannot be enslaved. In other words, the mind will always be free, regardless of the materials which enslave the body, be they stone walls or iron bars – his metaphors for the materials of imprisonment.

Perhaps such was reality in the 17th Century. Unfortunately, Lovelace could neither see the advent of computers and bioscience nor its potentially enslaving mechanisms. Nor was he as intuitively sentient as George Orwell and his concept of 'Big Brother' who would one day control the world. The alarming reality of today's world is that:

Computer walls can a prison make
and biochips a cage;
if modern man does not awake,
he'll suffer slavery's rage.

In search of ease and comfort
and blind to what *is* free,
man will shun discomfort
and forsake his liberty.

No body chained; no lashes felt;
his bondage, never sees;
but as he plays the cards he dealt,
he'll do so on his knees.

King

Tied and bound to techno strings,

a puppet slave to bio steel,

Freedom cannot spread her wings

lashed to a micro wheel.

The Biochip

Intrusions and invasions into the lives of all of us 'others' – common, ordinary, everyday people – continue to proceed unabated. One of the most frightening, if not *the* most frightening development in this regard, is the creation of the biochip – an electronic chip made from organic molecules rather than silicone or germanium, which can be implanted within animal and human bodies for purposes of monitoring and tracking. Such technology already exists and is actively being marketed. Touted as a means to insure the safety and convenience of others, such technology is a possible prelude to the enslavement of human beings on a scale unprecedented in human history. Of course in the promotion of the biochip or other similar species, human enslavement issues are not being mentioned, but the possibility of such bio-electronic incarceration is not only frightful but real, especially for freedom loving people who do not want to see their lives controlled by an all-seeing 'eye in the sky.'

This is not fiction. Dr. Rauni-Leena Luukanen-Kilde, former District Chief Medical Officer of northern Finland, has divulged the certainty of this reality in a

2000 article entitled: "*Microchip Implants, Mind Control and Cybernetics*" (microchip). For her bravery in unmasking this potential terror, she was given an award from CAHRA, Citizens Against Human Rights Abuse (Kilde). The following excerpts are from that article:

> #1. In 1948 Norbert Weiner published a book, Cybernetics, defined as a neurological communication and control theory already in use in small circles at that time. Yoneji Masuda, "Father of the Information Society," stated his concern in 1980 that our liberty is threatened Orwellian-style by cybernetic technology totally unknown to most people. This technology links the brains of people via implanted microchips to satellites controlled by ground-based supercomputers.

> #2. Today's supertechnology, connecting our brain functions via microchips (or even without them, according to the latest technology) to computers via satellites in the U.S. or Israel, poses the gravest threat to humanity. The latest supercomputers are powerful enough to monitor the whole world's population. What will happen when people are tempted by false premises to allow microchips into their bodies? One lure will be a microchip

King

identity card. Compulsory legislation has even been secretly proposed in the U.S. to criminalize removal of an ID implant.

#3. The mass media has not reported that an implanted person's privacy vanishes for the rest of his or her life. S/he can be manipulated in many ways. Using different frequencies, the secret controller of this equipment can even change a person's emotional life. S/he can be made aggressive or lethargic. Sexuality can be artificially influenced. Thought signals and subconscious thinking can be read, dreams affected and even induced, all without the knowledge or consent of the implanted person. (Kilde 2).

Surveillance Shackles

The biochip and its clones are not the only type of technological innovations warranting concern. Video surveillance cameras (literally everywhere now), ultra-wideband devices which can basically see through walls, face recognition apparatus, eye scans, infrared instrumentation, data collection methodologies and governmental laws allowing for the free exchange of personal information without individual consent all currently exist and are being used in various ways. The concern, of course, is whether these technologies will be abused or even nefariously used to surveil and ultimately subjugate the population at large, thus destroying their inherent freedom and individuality.

Perhaps one of its most concerning attributes is that the Two energy can be apathetic. As Helen Keller points out: "Science may have found a cure for most evils; but it has found no remedy for the worst of them all – the apathy of human beings" (Brainyquote, Keller).

This is one of the great concerns and dangers of this 2 Age of Others – people becoming so passive, apathetic, dependent and myopic that they relinquish control and responsibility of their own lives to a 'Big Brother' who *will* take control of them, give them the dependence they willingly choose and lead them summarily down the cotton candy propaganda path of pleasure, comfort and convenience right into the dark, dank, despicable den of abject slavery.

It would be foolish, if not totally purblind and ignorant, to think that such a state of affairs is not happening at this very moment. It definitely is happening but in ways that seem unobtrusive and non-alarming. In fact, the slavery that's ostensibly coming is being sold through the ideologies of ease, efficiency, convenience, public protection and increased standardization of living. Consider the immense daily data collection process that is literally amassing volumes of information on individuals – name, date and place of birth, street addresses, email addresses, phone numbers, fax numbers, medical history, vehicle ownership, educational history, employment history, marriages, divorces, credit card numbers, credit history, business and banking transactions and their histories, social security numbers and on and on and on. Think, too, of the number of cameras – visible and invisible – that monitor people's moves in banks, airports, stores, offices, elevators, street corners, amusement parks, stadiums, shopping centers, hospitals and schools. Reflect on how the technologies of retina/eye scan, credit card super cards, and the seldom mentioned and secretly promoted biochips, are being used or considered for use. All of these mechanisms have their positive aspects, but their flip side is more than negative, it's nefarious, and it's potentially enslaving.

Imagine your every move, action, thought, whereabouts, financial transaction, conversation, romantic liaison, recreation and entertainment activity being monitored by some all-seeing eye in the sky. With such surveillance, freedom would cease to exist. Life may be comfortable because someone else would be in charge, someone else would be making decisions for you, someone else would be telling you where to go, what to do, how to think. You wouldn't have to be responsible for yourself because someone else would be responsible for you. You wouldn't have to be independent because you would be totally and inescapably dependent. Life would be easy, comfortable, pleasurable, but you would be a slave – with absolutely no freedom, no liberty, no independence, no right to choose, no right to do anything except that which is approved by Big Brother or Big Sister or Big Daddy or Big Mama or Big Whoever.

Some may consider this concept paranoid. Is it? Are you sure? Who's calling people paranoid – the ones who are mastering the plan and designing the machinery of incarceration? It would not be the millionth time a strategy of attacking the other side to prevent one's intentions from being divulged or exposed was utilized. Is it the ones who love their life of ease and comfort and do not care about their freedoms as long as they are cared for, protected and living well who are concerned about this issue? Is it the ones who cannot recognize the onslaught of emerging patterns or the ones who are just too blind to see the truth?

Paranoia involves an extreme and unrealistic distrust of others. If people cannot, in fact, be trusted extremely, then there is no paranoia; there is simply the fact that people cannot be trusted. In consideration of a state of technological slavery, all that is necessary to realize its potential manifestation is to look at the progressions of mankind, the technological developments of the last hundred years, as well as the public's growing interest in the personal lives of other people and then extrapolate. Throw into this equation man's intense need for ease, comfort and pleasure and

King

there exists a definite recipe for mass control and enslavement of some sordid variety or another. People of his day may have thought George Orwell was paranoid when he wrote *1984* but was he? The obvious realities of the current age corroborate his suppositions.

Shackles of Plastic

In corroboration of the possibility of a Big Brother reality, an article by Karen Hube published in the Spring of 2003 on the moneycentral.msn.com website (no longer available) sends a portentous omen. Hube states:

> A cashless world is coming – just a lot later than we expected – and it's going to revolve around single plastic cards that provide currency, identification, security clearance and a whole lot more.

"Super cards" is the title given to the new generation of plastic infusing our society, instruments designed to make our lives easier, more convenient, more efficient by supporting multiple applications. Among their functions, such cards will not only replace cash, they will store all kinds of data and personal information as well as acting as security passes. How easy is life becoming. Right? To have one card do it all is amazing. But what 'all' is it doing or is it capable of doing? That's the nefarious rub.

The Age of the Female: A Thousand Years of Yin

Once the smart card is established, wouldn't the next step for 'convenience sake' be to simply do away with the nuisance of having to carry a card? After all, carrying a card is cumbersome, inconvenient and not as efficient as simply implanting a microchip in the hand or under a fold in the forehead. How easy. How convenient. How efficient. How simple. How enslaving! How scary!

Once a chip is implanted within a human body, manacles of a type previously unknown in human history will chain man as never before. Buying into the hype, spin and propaganda of ease, convenience, safety and efficiency, man will forfeit his freedom, sacrifice his safety and cement his slavery. His prison will not be one of stone walls and iron bars but microchips, supercomputers and an invisible watchdog warden of insidious intent. In all that he does, man will be controlled, monitored, manipulated. The only freedom he will have will be the freedom to conform and obey or be prey to a predator who seeks absolute subservience.

With all of the technological invasion into our personal lives, why are we not more concerned with such intrusions as supercards, supercomputers and super biochips? Do we not see? Do we not care? Do we neither know nor realize the dangers before us? Or are we simply setting the stage for the drama to come? Is the pendulum swinging from the polarity of freedom to that of slavery? Is the coin being flipped to its opposite side? Is day shifting into night? Is free thought and action

King

being replaced by controlled thought and conforming action? How right was George Orwell?

Core Millennia Shift

Timewise, it may appear that Orwell's predictions and intuitions of *1984* were incorrect. Actually, they were well within the framework of the Millennia Shift which began on 31 December 1957, the first "actual" natal vibration which equals 2000 (31 + 12 + 1957 = 2000). Thus, individuals born on this date were the first souls on the planet in recorded history to have the energy of the number 2000 anchored in their lives and charts (as the Actual Lifepath component). These individuals were vanguards heralding the oncoming millennium. Interestingly, just twelve weeks before the Millennia Shift began on Tuesday, 31 December 1957, the USSR had launched Sputnik into space on Friday, 4 October 1957 – a nano speck of cosmic time. You'll recall that Sputnik was the first artificial satellite to ever orbit the earth. It was earthman's first step into space, into the realm of other worlds. Coincidence? There are no coincidences in the universe. The synchronicity and precision of these two events and their corresponding dates defy normal explanation.

The core of the Millennia Shift began on 31 January 1969 and will not be completed until 31 December 2031, a period of sixty-three years. The first date creates the first Crown Pinnacle (4th) equating to the number 2000

The Age of the Female: A Thousand Years of Yin

(day-31 plus year-1969) and the latter date creates the last Crown Challenge (4th) at the end of the 2031 calendar year (year-2031 minus day-31 = 2000). Beginning on 1 January 2032 all the souls born on planet earth will, from that moment forward, have their major numerology timelines specifically anchored in 2 energy as reflected in the Epoch, Pinnacle and Challenge components of the "Life Matrix". This sixty-three year period is the most intense period of the millennia transition and is referred to as the *Core Millennia Shift*. After this core shift, it will take a full generation for those born prior to the core shift's end to run the course of their lives. Thus, although the stage is being set for Big Brother, the heart of the play, if there is to be such a drama, will not kick into high gear until the 22nd Century where the *master builder* cipher "22" will be activated in a process of order, structure, rules, regulations, regimes, security, stability and possible constriction and confinement. By then the mass consciousness will be saturated with 2 energy and the freedom fires of independence and individuality will have waned substantially, that is unless there is an awakening as to the importance of keeping freedom alive and avoiding the incarcerating shackles of apathy.

PEACE vs. PASSIVITY

The number 2 rules opposites. It also rules balance, the point of equilibrium between opposites. Balance is

King

critical to life, and when there is balance, there is peace. Where there is imbalance, there is chaos.

Because 2 rules peace and passivity, it is easy to make the mistake of thinking that peace is passivity. Nothing could be further from the truth. Peace is not passivity. Peace is an active state of balance between the opposing polarities of activity and passivity. If peace is defined as passive and passivity gains a foothold in the mass consciousness as equating to peace, the Age of Others will be ripe for the destruction of freedom and the construction of slavery.

Because peace is a midpoint between polar opposites, sometimes being passive is the answer to creating peace if the pendulum swings too far to the active pole. The reverse is also true. If the pendulum swings too far to the passive pole, then an adequate amount of activity must be generated to bring the passive energy into stasis.

Take, for example, the disease of cancer. It grows passively. When discovered, the remedies for its cure are quite active and sometimes violent. Surgery, chemotherapy and radiation treatment are often necessary to destroy the cancer and return the body to a peaceful, healthful state. None of these remedies is a passive countermeasure. They are extremely proactive, even violent. Yet, they are sometimes the only way to preserve life, and anyone who has ever known a friend who has undergone such treatment can acknowledge that the cancer patient was, in fact, fighting for his very life. Living passively under such conditions would not yield positive results. Therefore, passivity is not always the answer. In the case of fighting disease, activity is.

So it is with peace. Sometimes one must fight to preserve it, even die for it, as countless souls can testify. One of the concerns of the 2nd Millennium is that peace will become defined as passivity and people will forget how to fight in order to keep peace truly alive. Being passive in the face of cancer would spell certain death, just as being passive in the face of technological tyranny will spell certain death for freedom and liberty. Peace at any price is not peace, it is slavery, and those who choose peace and freedom must never forget that both are bought with a price, and that price is vigilance, not negligence; discipline, not dissipation, control, not indulgence; courage, not cowardice; activity, not passivity, and involvement, not apathy.

To prove the reality of dynamic activity in the peace process, try balancing on one foot with your eyes closed, or for an increased challenge, try balancing on an inflatable disk or balance board. Such a simple exercise verifies that creating a balanced state *and* maintaining it takes extreme concentration, work, skill, determination and strength. Balance is difficult, but without balance there can be no peace, which is why balance is primary and sacrifices must be made not only to achieve it but maintain it.

King

FREEDOM

Freedom is a great and wondrous thing. Unfortunately, until we lose something, we often do not appreciate its true value, and then it is too late to regain it and we are forced into deep remorse and regret. Freedom – the capacity to exercise choice – is often misunderstood and taken for granted, especially in free societies. Freedom is usually defined as 'license carte blanche' or choice without consequence. However, in a dual dimension of action and reaction there can be no choice without consequence. Hence, freedom must be defined as choice in consideration of consequence. Nothing is free. Everything has its price.

The price of freedom is discipline, self-control, sacrifice, temperance, awareness, obedience and vigilance. In consideration of its immense value and impending peril, the following quotations from famous historical figures are offered for introspection.

Freedom Quotes

Benjamin Franklin	They that can give up essential liberty to obtain a little temporary safety deserve neither liberty nor safety (Franklin).
Thomas Jefferson	I predict future happiness for Americans if they can prevent the

government from wasting the labors of the people under the pretense of taking care of them (Jefferson).

Douglas
MacArthur

No man is entitled to the blessings of freedom unless he be vigilant in its preservation (MacArthur).

Dwight
Eisenhower

If all that Americans want is security they can go to prison. They'll have enough to eat, a bed and a roof over their heads. But if an American wants to preserve his dignity and his equality as a human being, he must not bow his neck to any dictatorial government (Eisenhower).

George Orwell

War is peace. Freedom is slavery (Orwell).

Thomas Paine

Those who expect to reap the blessings of freedom must undergo the fatigue of supporting it (Paine).

Ronald Reagan

Freedom is never more than one generation away from extinction. We didn't pass it to our children in the bloodstream. It must be fought for,

King

protected, and handed on for them to do the same, or one day we will spend our sunset years telling our children and our children's children what it was once like in the United States where men were free (Reagan).

Woodrow Wilson   The history of liberty is the history of resistance (Wilson).

It is such a passion for freedom that will hopefully save the day and thwart the surge of bioslavery and Big Brother. The question is, "Will there be enough souls who understand the gravity of current circumstances to turn the tide and insure liberty throughout the Age of Others? Or will it simply be in mankind's common destiny to be enslaved and thus learn the hard lessons involved in creating and perpetuating freedom – lessons of awareness, sacrifice, discipline, control and struggle? Will man, in fact, continue to create freedom or will he be freely doomed?

RESPONSIBILITY vs. IRRESPONSIBILITY

True story. A high school student is told by his mother in the morning to get up, get dressed and eat breakfast so he can catch the school bus. Defiantly, he says, "No. I'm sleeping in." The mother retorts that if he doesn't get up, he'll have to walk to school, a distance of some four miles. He sleeps in. When he awakes, he demands his mother drive him to school because he missed the bus. She denies him. Bravo for her. Therefore, the young man is forced to walk four miles to school, whereupon he goes straight into the principle's office and files child abuse charges against his mother! Unbelievable! This is a young man who has rejected responsibility and accountability and made others not only responsible for his wrong doing but liable for any hardship he has to undergo because of his own indolence and negligence. And the fact that someone would defend the child in such circumstances undermines the qualities of self-responsibility, personal accountability and parental authority. Something like this never would have happened in yang years, but such things are happening today. It seems as though the compass of self-responsibility and personal accountability has been discarded.

This story highlights one of the major concerns of this age – individuals not taking responsibility for their own behaviors but laying the blame on others for their misdeeds. Unfortunately, they are getting away with such conduct. How come? In the case mentioned above, why would anyone even entertain the idea of accepting a child abuse claim against a parent who rightfully disciplined their child appropriately, setting him straight that he's responsible for his behavior and if he chooses differently there will be consequences to pay. So what if

King

he had to walk four miles to school? Maybe the next morning he'd get out of bed and catch the school bus like any self-responsible, self-accountable person would and should do.

Again the question is, "How come people are not being made to own up to their own behaviors in today's world?" Is the answer that as a society we've become too soft, too blind to the principle of self-responsibility and accountability that we blame anyone and everyone for our failings? Have we lost sight of the fundamental principles of life? Are we afraid to discipline ourselves? Are we apprehensive about disciplining anyone, to teach them what is acceptable and unacceptable? Or have we reached a place where we have lost our ethics compass, like our freedom compass, and we are just plain lost? Or are we simply careless?

The condition in our society today of people being made responsible for the actions of others is almost to the point of absurdity. How does a person, for example, purchase coffee through the drive-up window of a fast food restaurant, drive off, spill the coffee on herself and then sue the restaurant as if it were its fault, receiving a million dollar settlement in the process? How do a mother and father send their child under the protection of two nannies to a party in which the child drowns and the parents sue the host for millions of dollars, as if it were the host's fault, not the nannies who were given the task of caring for the child? Why should an airline be sued

The Age of the Female: A Thousand Years of Yin

simply because a parent felt offended by a flight attendant saying to some children, "Eenie, meenie, mynee, moe, take a seat we've gotta go?" Why is such ridiculous and frivolous litigiousness allowed to take even one breath, let alone survive and thrive? Most people who have any iota of common sense and sense of values are shaking their heads in total exasperation saying, "Please, please, please! would people get real?" It would not be surprising in today's reason-challenged environment if a lawsuit were filed simply because someone was offended and emotionally distraught because someone else used their finger to wipe the corner of their mouth rather than a napkin or brushed their hair with their hand rather than using a comb or brush. In light of the nonsensical atmosphere of our 'civilized' culture, it would not be unrealistic to conceive of someone being sued simply for taking a breath.

Obviously, the issues presented in the above examples, as well as addressing self-responsibilities, also address over-sensitivities. It is a sign of the times, an over-correction of 2 energy. Hopefully, clear and sane heads will ultimately prevail.

On the issue of responsibility, Barbara Jordan, U.S. Congresswoman from 1972-1978 and the first African-American to give a keynote address to the Democratic National Convention (Jordan 1), poignantly shares this thought: "We must exchange the philosophy of excuse – what I am is beyond my control – for the philosophy of responsibility" (Jordan 2). This is excellent advice for a generation which seems to moving away from its common sense, away from not only what is right but what is truly important, and few things are more important for a well-functioning society than its individuals taking responsibility for their actions.

MEDIOCRITY

One of the most accomplished women of the 20th Century was anthropologist Margaret Mead. She once stated, "Women want mediocre men, and men are working to become as mediocre as possible" (Mead). If this statement is true, it's definitely not a flattering commentary for women or men. It also did not originate from a flippant or flaccid mind. Margaret Mead was an extremely bright woman and the most famous anthropologist in the world at the time of her death in 1978. Her work spanned many cultures and encompassed subjects such as race relations, gender roles, self empowerment, child rearing, education, environmental justice, health and nutrition.

It would be interesting to poll today's women to see if they thought Mead's opinion was fair. Do women really want mediocre men? If so, why? Why desire something average? Is it simply a reflection of that side of the 2 that seeks to be like all others rather than striving to be unique, different and a-typical like the 1? Does it empower females to want mediocre males?

The Age of the Female: A Thousand Years of Yin

Does it level a playing field which has traditionally been male dominated? Why desire mediocrity in the first place? Why not desire excellence?

And why are men working to become as mediocre as possible, according to Mead? Do men no longer want to achieve? Have they lost their intrinsic drive for attainment and distinction? In their desire for women are men therefore aligning themselves with mediocrity just to get a woman? One can only hope Margaret Mead's observation does not maintain significant truth for the years ahead. If so, how sad for the world that it seeks common, ordinary ground rather than the exhilaration of the high road.

Mead's comment does strike a cord, though. Take virtue for example. Why is it denigrated so in our society? Do we no longer believe in purity of thought and behavior? When the subject of sexual abstinence among teens is mentioned as a means of controlling the spread of sexually transmitted diseases and childhood pregnancy, a common response is, "It's just not realistic." Why is that? Why is it not realistic for teens to be sexually abstinent? Are they so lacking in discipline that they are incapable of controlling themselves? Or have we as a society so immersed ourselves in sexual energy that we have misplaced the spiritual perspective of self-discipline and chastity?

Famous Twentieth Century choreographer and dancer Martha Graham beautifully noted, "The body is a sacred garment" (Graham). Have we lost sight of this fact? Have we discarded our inherent divinity?

There is a saying: "Argue for your limitations and they're yours." Is this not what we are doing today as far as the principles of excellence of character and spirit are concerned? Are we not limiting ourselves by arguing for our human failings and limitations instead of striving to achieve higher standards of moral and ethical behavior? It's commonplace today to mock virtue, as if such mockery were cool, and while ridiculing higher states of being may draw laughs, claps and cheers from some, such ridicule is a mediocre behavior at best. Comedienne Lily Tomlin once said: "Sometimes I worry about being a success in a mediocre world" (Tomlin). Sobering concern.

Man is bound by his thoughts and desires. If he sows the seeds of a low life, that's precisely what he will get. If he sows the seeds of an evolved life, he will ultimately achieve it. The fact is, we harvest what we plant and we cannot harvest what we do not plant. Let us hope and pray that this age does not fall prey to the madness of mediocrity. Such a disease would not be good for the health or progress of our civilization. Perhaps it might be wise to remember the words of French Nobel Laureate in Literature, Albert Camu: "Virtue cannot separate itself from reality without becoming a principle of evil (Camu).

The Age of the Female: A Thousand Years of Yin

DUPLICITY & DECEIT

One of the potential dangers of this new age is the expansion of duplicity and deceit. When the 2 energy slips too far to its own negative pole it becomes devious and manipulative, often pretending one set of feelings while acting under the influence of another. In other words, 2 can have dual faces, dual intentions. It can be smiling on the outside but sneering on the inside; truthful on the exterior, lying on the interior; one face for this person, another face for that person; a kiss on the cheek, a stab in the back. Hidden agendas are part of this paradigm.

It is this duplicitous aspect of the 2 that raises concerns for the future. Will dishonesty and deceit become the norm? Will individuals forego being forthright in their dealings with others in order to serve their own self interests? Will there be such a manifestation of deceitful behavior across the board that members of our society become benumbed and complaisant, thus allowing deceitfulness to grow and gain an even deeper foothold? Will people care about a direct approach at all, and will the act of being candid be out of vogue?

Take contracts for example. Where does there exist a simple, straight forward, clearly understandable contract without the fine, i.e., deceptive, small print? Why do contracts have to have fine print in the first place? Isn't such a practice deceitful prima facie? It would not be hard to argue the case that more contracts today are designed to deceive than openly declare truth.

How about marketing strategies? Who is there who has not fallen prey to the deceitful slogans and promises of companies which clearly do not deliver what they say they will? Is it not commonplace to distrust a used-car salesman or a mechanic? How about telemarketers? Online business opportunities? Who is there in today's world who tells the truth openly and clearly without having intricate, devious designs and self-serving agendas? Where are the straight shooters?

Then there's the scourge of spam. How intrusive and deceitful is this deplorable use of technology? If there were respect for other people's rights, spam would never exist. And if spam were not enough, what about spyware? Where is the permission to invade one's personal space and life? This type of infringement without consent is unacceptable and, frankly, unethical. The problem is that it's being accepted as if it were the norm. Individuals have a right to privacy and when that privacy is invaded without permission and/or announcement, there is an unadulterated assault on all things moral and ethical.

TERRORISM

The most negative expression of deceit, duplicity and indirectness is terrorism. It is, without a doubt, the plague of the age, a heinous manifestation of the worst characteristics of 2 energy and the one which warrants the greatest concern and danger because, unlike bioslavery, terrorism could well destroy the world, not just enslave it.

Terrorism is, of course, rooted in senseless killing in order to strike fear into people. But for what purpose? Hate? Revenge? Ego gratification? Disruption? Power plays? All of the above? Whatever the reasons, there are no good ones.

Terrorism is the pinnacle of iniquitous indirection. Cowardly reprehensible, it slithers under the surface of open and honest disagreement, hides behind misguided ideologies of religious and political benevolence, sacrifices the sanctity of human life in wicked ways, undermines the structure of a civilized society, defiles that which is pure and desecrates all that is holy. Its perpetrators are void of both humanity and spirituality, misguided miscreants who belong more to the underworld than the higher world and shall, no doubt, through the administration of spiritual law, one day be involuntarily forced to personally harvest the sinister and destructive seeds they have heinously sewn.

Unfortunately, terrorism is most likely to be with us for a while. The 2nd Millennium is, after all, just beginning and there are negative aspects to it just as there are positive ones. Notwithstanding its external evils, the underlying causes of terrorism will have to be addressed. How does one deal with hate, jealousy, anger, vengeance, religious and philosophical extremism in an age where openness is on the decline and indirectness, as well as global tensions, on the incline? Perhaps the silver lining will be in the ability of the world community to band together, lay aside ideological differences and do what the 2 energy does best . . . cooperate.

CHAPTER NINE

POSITIVES & PLUSES

Perfect helper, partner, mate,
Yin lives to balance and equate;
Forsaking one, embracing two,
for her relationship is true.
Her realm is others, tied, entwined –
Her loving legacy for all mankind.
Intuition is her natural season –
adjunct to the realm of reason.
Hidden secrets come to rise
within the glow of Yinlit skies.
Yin arms unfold to enfold peace;
caring tears which never cease.
Endearing love both near and far,
her dream – to light another's star.
Never one to laud herself,
Yin limelight rests upon the shelf.
The model father, friend and mother,
her every breath – to help another.
Sensitive in stormy weather,
Yin's always one to be together.

King

> Devoted, loving, start to end –
>
> positive pluses of the Yin.
>
> It *is* Her time. Watch her ascend
>
> as her kites rise against the wind.
>
> For a thousand years her ship *will* sail.
>
> Make no mistake, *she will* prevail.

The positive potentials of the Age of the Female rest in the achievement of balance in all things. What more could one hope for in a dimension of duality? The ceaseless shifting of the cosmic pendulum between polar opposites makes it difficult for any of us, let alone the global community, to create and maintain the equilibrium needed for a peaceful life. Yet, if man is to find happiness, he must first establish peace within himself. This is the great challenge of the Yin and her age, and if anyone can do it, she can.

Why her? Why can the Yin establish peace? Because she is the energy of peace. Intrinsically, she carries within her bosom and her womb energies of both the yin and yang. Yang is yang alone, but Yin is both. Therefore, knowing both gives her the capability of establishing a point of stasis between the two extremes.

Yin is the great equalizer, negotiator, diplomat. Her energy is not for herself, but for others. In her heart of hearts she wants to help, not hinder. She chooses not to lead but let others stand on her shoulders who would lead so they may be seen from afar. The limelight for her is witnessed in her glowing reflection of the ones she loves, and if she sits upon a throne it is a throne made for two, for her kingdom lies in relationship, partnership and togetherness, not monarchy. As a matriarch, her arms are always unfolding to enfold others in the warmth of an emotional embrace, and her intuition reaches insightfully into the depths of the psyche where reason cannot go. Hidden treasures and mysteries long submerged rise to the surface through her bipolar energy to gain exposure as she reveals the other side of life, thus creating a condition for all things to be brought into balance. Yin is not the conqueror but the companion who shares and cares for all who fall within the radiance of her touch. To be sure, if peace is attainable, its time is now, and if it can be attained and maintained, it will be the greatest and grandest legacy of the Age of the Female, the Age of Others.

If any of us truly wants peace, we must *live* peace. The same holds true for the world: if it wants peace, it must live it, not talk it. Killing or terrorizing to promote peace won't work any more than screaming at a deaf man to make him move. And with human life being held in such low regard by some people in this world, the probability of establishing peace on a global basis anytime soon is wishful thinking, to say the least. Therefore, if an individual desires to have a peaceful, harmonious life, he must create it within himself first, not wait for it to manifest in the outside world. Everything starts with the self.

Peace is an internal state. One can stand in the middle of a multitude of agitated souls and be at peace. Contrarily, he can be surrounded by a cavalcade of angels and be disturbed. Peace has nothing to do with what's *without*. It has everything to do with what's *within*.

A DIET FOR PEACE

We reap the deeds as we sow the seeds. It is the inescapable law of this creation. If we want peace, we must plant it because we cannot harvest what we do not plant. This peace-seeding begins, in part, at the core of our physical selves, our diet.

We are what we eat. This is another fact of life applicable to every one of us. As a general rule, if we eat lots of fat, we get fat. If we eat lots of vegetables and fruits, we stay lean. If we eat substances toxic to our bodies, we get sick; ingest too many, we die. Body composition and condition have definite causes. Likewise, peace has definite causes. One definitive cause creating the effect of peace rests in the food we eat. Look at the following list of people. It's an impressive catalogue. All of the souls on this list have something in common. What is it?

Sir Isaac Newton	Pythagoras	Albert Einstein
Gautama the Buddha	Mohandas Ghandi	Mother Teresa
Plato	Plutarch	Socrates
Leonardo da Vinci	Vincent Van Gogh	St. Francis of Assisi
Albert Schweitzer	Charles Darwin	Leo Tolstoy
Susan B. Anthony	George Bernard Shaw	Queen Sophia of Spain
Henry David Thoreau	Ralph Waldo Emerson	Louisa May Alcott
H.G. Wells	Dr. Benjamin Spock	Mr. (Fred) Rogers
Paul McCartney	Linda McCartney	Ringo Starr
John Lennon	Yoko Lennon	George Harrison

King

Coretta Scott King	Billie Jean King	Shania Twain
Joan Baez	Bob Barker	Doris Day
Dennis Weaver	Richard Gere	Leonard Nimoy
Dwight Yoakam	K. D. Lang	Carl Lewis
Mary Tyler Moore	Kim Basinger	Gloria Steinem
Martina Navratilova	Stephanie Powers	Woody Harrelson

Extraordinary list, isn't it? Frankly, it's incomplete. It could be much larger. However, for the purposes of this book, propriety mandates brevity. In fact, there are hundreds of millions of people who, although not famous, also share what the people on this list share. What is it that binds them all together? Is it occupation? No. Gender? No. Age? No. Nationality? No. Geography? No. Language? No. Time period in which they lived? No. Financial status? No. The common thread binding these souls together is their diet – they're all vegetarians (famousveggie)!

What's notable in the above list is that it's comprised mostly of ordinary people who have done

The Age of the Female: A Thousand Years of Yin

extraordinary things and, of course, all of the people on the list maintain some type of celebrity status. But what is impressive about the list is that mystics throughout the ages such as Guru Nanak, Kabir, Hafiz, Namdev, Tukaram, Charan Singh, Shams-I-Tabriz, Dadu, Paltu, Dariya, Rumi, Jagat Singh, Ravidas, Mira Bei, Seth Shiv Dayal, Baba Ji Maharaj, Sawan Singh, Sahjo Bei, Buella Shah, Tulsi Das, Ram Das, Guru Arjun, Gobind Singh, Amar Das and Teg Bahadur are not on the list. Yet, they were all vegetarians. They were all perfect, realized souls of the highest order, and one would naturally expect them to be vegetarians because of their exalted spiritual status. If they were the only ones comprising such a list, it wouldn't be a surprise at all, but when ordinary people become vegetarians, in the millions, it is noteworthy.

In the millions? Yes. India alone, for example, has approximately one billion people, hundreds of millions of whom are vegetarian, probably more than the entire population of the United States. Still, the number of vegetarians in America is growing, as reflected in the number of vegetarian products now available in supermarkets compared to just twenty years ago. In 1980 there were few products serving vegetarians. Now grocery stores are not only filled with vegetarian products, but rows of them. Soy protein, as one illustration, is being developed into faux burgers, ribs, chicken, sausage, turkey, cheeses and a whole myriad of tasty delights. Were the numbers of vegetarians not increasing, businesses certainly wouldn't be developing these new products which are being fueled by demand, purely and simply. If there were no demand for them, businesses wouldn't lift a finger to produce them. But that's not the case. The demand for vegetarian foods is growing daily. Ask any long-standing vegetarian. Ask the grocer. To be sure, vegetarianism is on the rise.

What is a vegetarian? A vegetarian is one who abstains from eating the flesh of living beings. In other words, nothing that ever had a heartbeat, a face or a mother. There are basically three types of vegetarians: vegan, lacto and ovo-lacto. Vegans (generally pronounced "vee-gun") eat no animal products whatsoever. Lacto-vegetarians allow themselves dairy but no eggs, egg-whites or products containing them such as mayonnaise, animal gelatin, beef or chicken-based broths and soups, condiments and sauces containing animal products or anchovies. Ovo-lacto vegetarians may consume eggs and dairy. However, in no case does a vegetarian eat animal flesh. If one abstains from red meat but eats fish and/or chicken, he is not a vegetarian. Fish and chicken are still flesh. Such a person simply follows a diet devoid of red meat but that does not qualify him as being a vegetarian.

Why is a vegetarian diet gaining popularity? For many reasons. Health issues certainly play a role. Spiritual, religious and philosophical interests provide a major consideration. Economic and environmental concerns are also germane because the growing of crops is a more efficient use of land for feeding people than is the grazing of livestock. Will all the people in the world become vegetarians? Most likely not. But their numbers are growing, to be sure, and they will continue to grow as the consciousness of life expands.

The core reason for vegetarianism is compassion for all life. It's a safe bet that the overwhelming majority of vegetarians are against the killing of animals simply to provide food for themselves. Why kill? Why destroy? Why slaughter animals to eat their flesh when there is a plethora of non-animal alternatives available in today's world? All spiritual scriptures and saints have decried killing and that includes the killing of animals, not just humans. If one is truly spiritually inclined, this statement must give one pause.

In consideration of the law of cause and effect, a vegetarian diet is mandatory if one desires peace. There is simply no other choice. We reap what we sow; we harvest what we plant. How can we reap peace when we plant violence? How can we harvest life when we plant death? Killing begets killing. How can we preach peace and profess love when we engage directly or indirectly in the murder of living beings? How can we express life if we're putting death in our bodies?

The soul is the essence of God, the life force, so by taking life, by killing, we are not only desecrating that

King

which is holy and sanctified but also desecrating God Himself. And since God is love, when we kill living beings, we kill love. Where there is no love, there can never be peace.

CHRIST AS A VEGETARIAN

When we think of the divine diet of vegetarianism, we think of divine souls, spiritual souls, souls living, breathing and expressing the God Force. This, of course, begs the question, "Was Jesus the Christ a vegetarian?" In answering this controversial question, let's recall some of the famous historical figures who have been vegetarians: Pythagoras, Mohandas Gandhi, Albert Schweitzer, Leonardo de Vinci, St. Francis of Assisi, Aristotle, Plato, Socrates, Mother Teresa, George Bernard Shaw, Paul McCartney.

The reputations of these souls, as well as others, are well known. They were individuals of extreme accomplishment and clearly distinguished themselves as exceptional human beings exuding an extreme sensitivity to life, its quality and consciousness. It is safe to say that these notable individuals not only attained enormous status in their fields and in their stature among humanity, but they also expressed a relatively high level of enlightenment. Yet, it is also probably safe to say that compared to Jesus the Christ, they were not as evolved spiritually. So . . . the question must be asked: "If these great and evolved souls were vegetarians, if they chose not to kill, slaughter, and eat the flesh of animals because of their own elevated state of human consciousness, their tender-heartedness, and their disdain for destruction, if they were able to connect the dots between an enlightened life of compassion and its dietary regimen, how could one such as Christ – so much more highly evolved – express lesser thought and action by killing and eating flesh?" Thus, the issue is not whether Jesus was or was not a vegetarian. The question is, "How could Christ possibly not have been vegetarian?"

Besides these greatly distinguished historical personages, there have been and currently are millions of souls on this planet, human and animal, who are also vegetarians. In fact, some of the biggest and strongest creatures on the earth are in this category – elephants, oxen, gorillas, giraffes, horses and cattle. Why would millions of souls throughout time, souls who are living and have lived on this little insignificant planet, choose not to eat meat? Furthermore, given the absolute numbers of beings who by instinct and choice have chosen not to eat animal flesh, how could a professed Son of God do otherwise? It makes absolutely no sense whatsoever. If we take a simple, cursory look at the nature of Jesus the Christ, we see an extremely evolved soul, a Son of God who loved and *lived* love. He was kind, kingly, divine. His life's work was about elevating the consciousness of those souls who followed him. It was not about killing, hurting, maiming, destroying, creating pain and suffering for its own sake. It was about saving souls, severing their attachment to this world and liberating them from the bondage of this earth. In his book, *The Lost Religion of Jesus* (Lantern Books, New York), Keith Akers explores the reality of Christ being a vegetarian, joining the ever-growing legion of historians and theologians who share the same belief (Akers).

Furthermore, Jesus not only knew the Great Law of cause and effect, of karma, he taught it. It was his interpretation of the Law of Compensation and Adjustment as that of sowing and reaping that is still with us today. He believed in the commandments of not killing, not committing adultery, fornicating, stealing or hurting others. Here was a grand Soul who preached that the meek shall inherit the earth. Here was a Son of God who taught that man cannot serve two masters – God and mammon. Here was a Divine Being whose life was about Light, not darkness; Life, not death; who taught that God is a Spirit and that the desires of the flesh were of the devil, the negative power. How in His Kingdom, therefore, could such a Son of God slay animals, eat their flesh and support the very force which he spent his entire life and lifeblood opposing? To reiterate, then, the germane question is not whether Jesus the Christ, Son of God, was a vegetarian. It is, most emphatically, "How could he not have been?"

The Age of the Female: A Thousand Years of Yin

INNER YIN

Another plus for the Age of the Female rests in the positive facet of its bipolar nature. As the yin rules that which is both positive and negative, it also governs that which is both internal and external. During the Age of the Male, the emphasis was on the external aspect of life – those things which can be perceived in the outer world of phenomena. But with the reversal of the cosmic pendulum, the energy shift is being directed to the internal world of its phenomena. Whereas before we lived from the outside in, now we have the opportunity to live from the inside out and establish a true sense of balance between inner and outer polarities.

What does this mean? Intuition and hidden knowledge will move to the forefront of our consciousness. We will have the opportunity to tap into and therefore follow and trust our "inner knowing" much more deeply and thoroughly than we have done in the past, at least collectively. The "still small voice" which speaks to us will neither be still nor small for those who become attuned to its vibration. Business decisions will no longer be exclusively based on a rational, linear line of mental processing. Deeper energies will be tapped, contacted and utilized in the management of our daily affairs. Learning to "listen" to the "voice" which speaks to us from within will be an emerging life-enhancing technique imminently practical during the next thousand years.

King

Because this age is concerned with that which lies beneath the surface, the knowledge to harmonize with all that lies below will expand and, like a magnet, draw our attention inward. Hidden secrets will therefore be revealed; mysteries, unknown to the masses of 1st Millennium Man, will rise to the surface for exposure and observation. People in general will become much more attuned to the inner realities of life and living. Perceptions will change. What was once commonly believed to be reality will morph into a totally different set of archetypes. Our "knowing" will not be strictly based on reason but something less concrete, more abstract, but still real. We will learn to trust a force we can neither see, touch, taste, or smell but which we can "feel" with our intuitive equipment and internal processors. If person A were to ask person B how he knows something, person B will say, "I don't know how I know. I just know." And he'll be right. Empirical knowing will give way to intuitive knowing during this Age of Others.

Traditional science will undergo a metamorphosis during the coming centuries. Physics – the study of the natural, material world of phenomena, will be joined by metaphysics – the science which explains and defines reality by going beyond (meta) the limitations established by an external perception of things and events. Where traditional science cannot go, non-traditional science will. Old truths may die hard, but they will still die. For the last thousand years science has only looked at one side of the life coin – that which can be measured externally. In the coming age it will get a chance to investigate the other side of the life-science coin – that which can only be experienced internally – and science might be startled at the findings.

As a case in point, the art and science of numerology will no doubt grow. Although of ancient origins and standing the test of time, its veracity in this current age may be challenged at first. As the great scientist, musician and philanthropist Dr. Albert Schweitzer said, "It is the fate of every truth to be an object of ridicule when it is first acclaimed" (Schweitzer). Nonetheless, there is far too much truth within the parameters of numerology to cast it aside as unworthy, unreal or unscientific. It has certainly not withstood time's tests for lacking credibility and substance. As a metaphysical science, numerology can be substantiated, corroborated, validated. It can, and does, explain many things about life which traditional science cannot explain. Numerology allows us to see beyond the veil of the external world and into the mysteries of the apparent unknown and ostensibly unexplainable world. When Pythagoras said, "Numbers rule the universe; everything is arranged according to number and mathematical shape," he wasn't simply referring to mathematical formulae. He was referring to life.

King

One such concept which numerology proves is that of predestination – the predetermination of life and its events. Most people today, especially those who believe that life is a random happening, will disagree. This is natural, but such belief does not invalidate the reality that the path we follow in life is a beautifully orchestrated divine design perceivable through our natal birth name and birth date. As Christ himself said (Bible: St. Matthew 10:30): "But the very hairs of your head are all numbered," a phrase corroborating the extensive establishment of a pre-determined outcome. As has already been substantiated, Einstein believed that "everything is determined" and a famous Indian maxim reiterates this truth: "On every grain (of rice), the name of the eater is written." (Langenkamp). Sawan Singh, a perfect master of the Twentieth Century stated, "Whatever is happening is all preordained" (Singh 2).

No doubt there will be other truths gaining exposure. It will be interesting in this next thousand years to see what rises to the surface from the depths of reality's hidden treasures. There is also no doubt that whatever rises will be both negative and positive because of the dual nature of this dimension, but when clouds come, they will all come with silver linings.

The Age of the Female: A Thousand Years of Yin

MEDITATION

Peace reigns within. Chaos rains without. Therefore, the more we move in an inward direction, the more peace and less chaos we experience. We also become more balanced in the process. Through meditation, our perspectives of life change. In fact, so do its realities. Mystics throughout the ages have taught that secret treasures, hidden mysteries, and celestial kingdoms lie *within* us, and if we venture 'In' we will definitely find them. Meditation is the vehicle of the inner journey.

In its highest sense, meditation leads us to oneness with God. In its beginning phase it is an exercise to help quiet the mind and relax the body. Meditation has levels, just like the educational system. The more skilled we become at it, the higher we advance. We learn, practice, test, graduate and move to the next level. Ultimately, meditation culminates in God Realization and liberation of the soul.

Meditation is a discipline. It is also a way of life. It is not an amusement. The argument can be made that meditation is life itself because without it we cannot advance spiritually. Meditation is an absolute requirement for the ascendancy of the soul. Without meditation the mind can never be stilled, tamed, slain and transgressed. It must be conquered because it is *the* great barrier to spiritual progress. The mind *is* the enemy, and until we still the mind we will not be able to perceive the Spirit Within, just as we cannot see our reflection in muddied, ruffled water. However, when water is perfectly still and pure, we can see our reflection in its mirror-like surface. Stillness through meditation then becomes a pre-requisite to spiritual ascent. Stillness creates the mirror of spiritual reflection and divine realization.

With the Age of the Female and its potential for balance and peace, the process of meditation becomes enhanced. Meditation is an internal activity, and since the 2 energy rules opposites, souls have a greater chance to move their attention inward, away from the chaotic turmoil of the outer world to the effulgence of the inner worlds.

Hurricanes offer us a great analogy in understanding this dualism. The external winds of a hurricane are fierce, tumultuous, and potentially lethal. As we get caught up in the whirlwinds and worldwinds of life, our lives become windswept and turbulent. It's impossible to experience any modicum of peace because the savage and relentless nature of the whirling winds circulating at a perilous pace keeps us imbalanced and in dire distress.

In stark contrast to the outer winds of the hurricane, the center of the hurricane, the eye, is relatively still, calm and cloud free – the exact opposite of the circling, cycling mayhem of winds existing in the outer perimeters of its wheel. As the 'eye' is at the center of the hurricane, we must move to the 'eye' of our own life. It is there we will find peace. We do this through meditation and, ironically, we do it through the 'Third Eye' mentioned extensively in mystical literature. It is through this aperture, this 'eye,' that we find a place of rest. Mystically, as we progress on our spiritual journey, we also find an interior passageway to the inner worlds, a sort of secret door leading to other dimensions, other realities. As Christ said in St. Luke 11:37, "The light of the body is the eye: therefore, when thine eye is single, thy whole body also is full of light." Notice the word is "eye" not eyes.

This fact of light being accessible through the 'single eye' is common to all mystical teaching, not just Christianity. When we move through this eye viz. a viz. the process of meditation, there is not only light, there is peace, calm, tranquility, and new realities to experience. As every cloud has its silver lining, so every one of life's hurricanes has its eye. It is there we need to go to find peace.

Arguably, the precise purpose of the storms and tempests of our lives is to move us inward to the eye of the storm where we can find tranquility. The goal of meditation is to still the mind; make it thoughtless. If we stubbornly remain within the framework of the mind's outer winds, we will experience only discord in life. But if we want peace, we must redirect our focus from the outer cravings of the mind and its desire for worldly allurements – the cause of its winds – to the inner realities of the spiritual path where we find stillness, peace, bliss and clear skies which give us clearer spiritual vision. The process for this is meditation.

Following a vegetarian diet is a wonderful adjunct to the meditative life. A more peaceful diet leads to a more peaceful mind. Eating meat involves us in acts of killing and violence, and when the winds of these actions come back around, they do so with like-kind vengeance. Murderous winds of action bring murderous winds of reaction. Poisonous seed gives poisonous fruit. Such is the law, and it is as inviolable as it is inescapable.

In fact, not just giving up eating meat but abstaining from alcohol and recreational drugs is equally important in being successful in meditation and, therefore, in creating peace. Such substances not only agitate the mind and keep it disturbed, they also keep its winds whirling and swirling, thus dulling the soul's ability to sense higher realities prevailing within the finer vibratory fields of the eye center. If we truly want peace, we must learn to be still. To be still, we must do those things which create stillness. Following a flesh-free, alcohol-free, drug-free, ethical life with regular meditation is a certain recipe for success in obtaining peace and making spiritual strides while living in the world.

Meditation takes work, just like anything. As it is impossible for a musician to create performance-caliber music without daily practice, sacrifice and discipline, so it is equally impossible for any of us to create stillness and peace without practicing daily meditation. Wishing won't work. Doing does. If we want peace, we have to create it. Creation means practice, sacrifice, discipline, dedication, determination, devotion, consistency and perseverance. If we sit around and wait for peace to come, it never will. We'll just keep being tossed about by the winds of our lives, suffering in the process. We must be proactive, learn to move to the center, to the eye of the storm, where there is peace.

How does one meditate? Techniques vary with advancement. Perfect mystics, for example, are the keepers of the meditative flame, the key to its secrets. As we progress in our spiritual journey, and if we are fortunate enough to meet such a realized soul, the higher secrets of meditation will be revealed to us. In the beginning, however, we need to work on our concentration. Here are a few exercises which may be helpful.

The Number Progression

Find a quiet place to sit where there are no distractions – no music, no television, no chatter. It's best not to have a full stomach. Close your eyes; be very still; keep from moving. Concentrate your attention at a point between the eyebrows.

King

With this preparatory work done, try to visualize the number 1. Say it mentally, then move to the number 2, then to 3 and so forth. Try to make it to 20. Here's the catch: if at any time you think of anything else or lose sight of the numbers during the process, you have to start over at number 1. Don't be surprised if you're not successful right away. The mind is very slippery; in fact, treacherous. That's its nature. That's its job. Odds are that somewhere along the line you'll find yourself thinking about a whole plethora of things from what you did or will do during the day to what you're going to eat when you get up, something somebody said to you, what's on television, etc. The list is endless. If and when you are successful counting to twenty, move to thirty, then to forty. Try to get to one-hundred. Keep attempting to push back your barriers and extend the degree and strength of your concentration. This exercise will demonstrate how difficult the mind is to control and therefore, the need to control it, discipline it, and make it subservient to your will, not its own. This will also demonstrate that there is something deeper than the mind, something that motivates you to control the mind. That something is the spirit. It must learn to do the controlling through the exercise of your will. Do not obey the dictates of the mind. Make it obey you. It is your servant. You are not its slave unless you submit to it and follow its dictates.

The Age of the Female: A Thousand Years of Yin

The Mystical Pond

This is a wonderful meditation for gaining peace and emotional control. First do the preparatory work: quiet place, no noises, distractions, be still, etc. After a few moments of quieting yourself, visualize a perfectly still pond with a surface so serene and glassy you can see your reflection in it, just as you would were you to look in a mirror. This pond you've created is mystical. Not only is it perfectly still, it maintains its own power/force shield. If some projectile were hurled toward the pond, the force shield would repel the projectile which would, therefore, never touch the surface of the water, keeping the water's surface perfectly serene and still. See this happen. Visualize something being thrown toward the pond but being deflected by the pond's invisible power shield. Note that nothing can upset the stillness of the water, nothing . . . ever. Time and time again as something is hurled toward the pond its force field rejects the object, protecting its glass-like surface.

Emotions are like water. When we establish an image of water being so still that nothing can disturb it, the image has the potential of keeping us calm when normal life disturbances assault our feelings and water-like emotions. With the vision of perfectly still water established in our minds, even subconscious minds, we are less apt to become disturbed and lose our sense of peace when some outside force is imposed upon us. We, therefore, remain calm, poised and in control of ourselves during the volatile vicissitudes of life.

The Secret Sanctuary

In your meditative space and place visualize a sparkling, pure white fortress in the sky, a place where you go to find rest and repose. The walls, the stairs, the furniture, everything about this coruscating castle is brilliant, protective, impregnable, surrounded by pure white light. This is your safe place, your secret sanctuary. Like the mystical pond, this ethereal citadel repels all negative winds with a power of such magnitude that whatever approaches it is instantly dissolved. This is God's gift to you, and other than you, only He may gain entrance. It is here you commune with Him because this secret hideaway is holy ground, immaculately pure and crystalline white – glistening, glowing and shimmering with super-natural power and protection. This is your sanctum sanctorum, the innermost shrine of your being. It is unbreakable and impregnable. It is your divine sanctuary.

There are an infinite number of such meditational images. These are given simply to encourage personal creativity and involvement in the process. Meditation is wellness engendering. As the Age of the Female runs its course, this devotional activity can no doubt serve to help create personal inner peace for those who use it.

The Age of the Female: A Thousand Years of Yin

And speaking of personal peace, isn't that one of the major goals in life? When we think about it, we really can't change another person. It's difficult enough to change ourselves, let alone someone else. Therefore, we should avoid the trap of trying to create a peaceful world by making everyone else conform to our specific set of religious, ideological, philosophical, psychological, governmental and economic criteria. Were everyone committed to creating peace in themselves first and foremost, the world would become a peaceful place automatically. Is it not better to let our own light shine and grow and thereby illuminate the darkness around our personal space rather than run around trying to light everyone else's candle at the risk of having our own candle's flame extinguished? Peace lies within, and peace, like charity, starts at home – the personal center of our being.

YIN IN HAND

One of the greatest pluses of the Age of the Female is the potential for cooperation and togetherness. The 2 energy is saturated with vibrations of others and relationship. This *is* the time to help one another. The exploration and conquest of the world has had its time. The exploration and conquest of human interaction and partnership is now the order of the day. Unquestionably, our human civilization can make great strides if we, as a world people, can learn to share and work together.

King

258

The virtues and attributes of equality, tolerance, tenderness, compassion, sweetness and genuine understanding are inherently magnetized in the energy of the 2. The key, however, is to allow these characteristics to flow naturally from person to person, country to country, without governmental regulation. People helping people; people sharing with people; people striving to establish a sense of community because they want to, not because they have to, are keys to creating a global legacy of historical substance and import. Compassion can't be legislated. Love is not a calculable commodity. Love simply gives without thought of return. Once it thinks of return, it is reduced to a simple business transaction. Lovers never calculate, they just give, just as the sun never calculates – it just shines.

Does one lose one's identity in partnership? No. It takes many individual pillars to support a roof. The crux is that the roof gets supported . . . equally. Networking in business is an excellent manifestation of this assistance principle. Ride sharing to work, car-pooling kids to after-school events, learning to give and take in personal matters, sharing jurisdiction in law enforcement cases, and governments working diligently to improve and insure the well-being of everyone do not mitigate individuality. Such activities rather honor individuality through personal sacrifice and sharing. In effect, yin-in-hand is working hand-in-hand with others to create a better world – personal or global.

The Age of the Female: A Thousand Years of Yin

YIN IN ASCENT

The yin energy is not exclusive to women. Men, too, fall within its vibrational aura. As the yin/yang symbol depicts a white dot within its black hemisphere and a black dot within its white hemisphere encapsulated within the confines of a circle and separated by a wavy line, so there is yang within yin and yin within yang in a circle of completeness separated by a fluid line insuring flexibility. Total separation and autonomy of either yin or yang is impossible in this world in which there is an inter-connection within all living things, both masculine and feminine. To deny either and proclaim the other is to deny both and claim neither. We are all parts of an inseparable whole in this world and none of us is more important to the whole than the other, which is why the establishment of peace is critical to our quality of life. Peace acknowledges, appreciates, respects, honors and extols both polarities of the life force. It is therefore essential for happiness.

How fortunate is earth to have a thousand years of yin! Balance is supreme in the quest for peace and without her energy flowing and following the yang age, there could not even be the hope of balance, let alone peace. We need yin, and we would be crazy not to embrace her. Fortunately for us, God has taken care of that, and the great cosmic pendulum has reversed its direction to bring yin into the drama. If Shakespeare were to write a play and call it "Yin & Yang", we would

King

now be in Act II, Scene 1. How appropriate is it that she, who is ruled by the number 2, would take center stage in Act II? It is all so perfect!

However, in order for yin to achieve the heights contained inherently within her energy field during her age, she must be diligently devoted to creating a state of balance, without which the lofty legacy of her beautiful being will be lost and never realized. She could easily crash and burn in a fireball of self-serving ego mania. Remember the 11 transition roots within her framework? They are powerful. Double fire. This could equate to the fire of inspiration or obliteration; the harmonious reality of peace and prosperity or the inharmonious actuality of war and destruction.

The saving grace is that in its highest and most edified expression, 2 is the vibration of caring, compassion, cooperation, understanding, tolerance, togetherness, brotherhood. The number 2 ties and binds. If it ties with love, how special can things be?

But what is love? It is that vibration which seeks the highest and best good for all living things. That highest and best good is God realization, not material saturation, personal self-service or individual aggrandizement. The 2 energy potentially shares and hordes. If it shares, there is no end to what it can accomplish. If it hordes, there are no depths to which it can sink. Within the grandest scope of the 2 energy, everyone must be taken care of.

Principally, the 2 is about others, not the self. The age of the self has passed. As we watch world events unfold, we will see this truth before our very eyes. The challenge now is integrating, caring for and balancing the needs of everyone. It is not about satisfying the desires of the few and the selfish. If the latter philosophy dominates and the internal pendulum of the 2 is allowed to sway to its self-serving polarity, there will be immense tension and conflict in the world. For its highest and best good to be made manifest, the 2 must share. That's what 2 does best. The 2 also inspires and cooperates to fulfill common goals. Underneath its surface, 2 is aflame with the fire of creativity, partnership, understanding, tolerance and peace. If that is the focus, such will be the reality. If that is what is planted on earth, then that is what will be harvested.

Though distinctly separate and oppositional in nature, yin and yang are deeply intertwined. One cannot exist without the other. Kites do need the wind's opposing forces to soar on high, just as chunks of coal need heat, pressure and time to become diamonds. The road to success is paved with failure, and the beauty of the rose is realized in juxtaposition with the weed. For us to know love, we sometimes have to experience hate by contrast. To appreciate peace it is often necessary to experience the tensions of confliction. We should, therefore, not be surprised if, during the initial one hundred years of the new millennium, situations and events arise in which contrasting opposites appear, setting the stage for positive yin energies to rise into the more noble skies of her destiny.

Yin is compassion. She is peace. She is balance. She is friend. The consummate helper and partner, yin strives to support others and share the wealth of life with all. This next millennium *is* her moment in the history of this earth, our world. The Age Of The Female, A Thousand Years of Yin, is now. May it be blessed with all the positives and pluses residing in her heart of hearts so that all living beings will prosper and be whole.

~ finis ~

WORKS CITED

Addams   Women's History. Jane Addams Quotes. 10 April
                         2006 <http://womenshistory.about.com/od/
                         quotes/a/jane_addams.htm>

AIDS   So Little Time: An AIDS History. 10 April
                         2006 <http://www.aegis.com/topics/
                         timeline/default.asp>

Ailor   Ailor, William. Email Interview. 30 December
                         2002

Akers   CompassionSpirit.com. Akers, Keith. The Lost
                         Religion of Jesus 16 April 2006 <http://
                         www.compassionatespirit.com/ Animal-
                         People-review.htm>

Aldrin   Global Icons. Buzz Aldrin. 7 April 2006
                         <http://www.globalicons.com/actors/
                         Aldrin/>

Anthony   History of the Susan B. Anthony Dollar
                         9 April 2006 <http://
                         www.direwolfauctions.com/
                         sbanthonydollarhistory.htm>

Archer   NBC News: The Funeral of Diana. August 1997

Armstrong   Biographies of U.S. Astronauts 7 April 2006
                         <http://www.spacefacts.de/english/
                         bio_ast.htm>

Banks   Banks, Kimberly J. "Stanton and Anthony
                         Papers Online Project." Diss. Rutgers U,
                         1999. 6 April 2006 <http://
                         ecssba.rutgers.edu/studies/
                         ecsbio.html>

Bella   BellaOnline: The Voice of Women. Helen Keller
                         Quotations. 12 April 2006 <http://
                         www.bellaonline.com/articles/
                         art14069.asp>

Berlin Wall   1. A Concrete Curtain: The Life and Death of
                         the Berlin Wall. 9 April 2006 <http://
                         www.wall-berlin.org/gb/berlin.htm>
                         2. Berlin Wall History 9 April 2006 <http://
                         www.dailysoft.com/berlinwall/>

Black Jack   Arlington National Cemetery Website. John
                         Fitzgerald Kennedy. 9 April 2006
                         <http://www.arlingtoncemetery.net/
                         jfk.htm>

Brainyquote,   Brainyquote.com. Churchill, Winston. 22 March
Churchill   2006 <http://www.brainyquote.com/quotes/
                         quotes/w/winstonchu125996.html>

Brainyquote, Davis   Brainyquote.com. Bette Davis Quotes. 11 April
                         2006 <http://www.brainyquote.com/quotes/
                         quotes/b/bettedavis133306.html>

Brainyquote, Keller   Brainyquote.com. Helen Keller Quotes. 12
April 2006 <http:// www.brainyquote.com/
quotes/quotes/h/helenkelle125476.html>

Camu   BrainyQuote.com. Albert Camus. 13 April 2006
<http://www.brainyquote.com/quotes/
authors/a/albert_camus.html>

Cold War   The Cold War Museum. Fall of the Soviet
Union. 9 April 2006 <http://
www.coldwar.org/articles/90s/>

Confucius 1   Brainyquote. Confucius Quotes. 11 April
2006 <http://www.brainyquote.com/quotes/
authors/c/confucius.html>

Confucius 2   Classical Library. The Analects: XX, 3.
11 April 2006 <http://
www.classicallibrary.org/
confucius/analects/20.htm>

Couteau, First Flight   Couteau, Robert. The Wright Brother's First
Flight. 1999 <http://members.tripod.com/
tra_nations/1e_wrights.htm>

Couteau, Orville   Couteau, Robert. The Wright Brother's First
Flight. 1999 <http://members.tripod.com/
tra_nations/1e_wrights.htm>

Couteau, Wilbur   Couteau, Robert. The Wright Brother's First
Flight. 1999 <http://members.tripod.com/
tra_nations/1e_wrights.htm>

Desert Storm   Operation Desert Storm: Chronology 9 April
2006 <http://www.desert-storm.com/War/
chronology.html>

Earhart   The Official Site of Amelia Earhart 7 April
2006 <http://www.ameliaearhart.com/>

Eisenhower   Dwight (Ike) Eisenhower, President 12 April
2006 <http://oaks.nvg.org/1g2ra3.html>

Famous Veggie   FamousVeggie.com. 16 April 2006 <http://
www.famousveggie.com/>

Figure 1   NASA. Apollo 11: 30th Anniversary 7 April
2006 <http://history.nasa.gov/
ap11ann/introduction.htm>

Figure 2   World Trade Center. Email, 2003
<http://www.advancedelec.com>

Figure 3   Petronas Twin Towers. The Petronas Corp.
Email, 2003 <http://www.petronas.com/
indexcorp.htm>

Franklin   The Quotations Page, Benjamin Franklin.
12 April 2006 <http://
www.quotationspage.com/quotes/
Benjamin Franklin/21>

Gagarin   Russian Archives Online. Yuri Gagarin: His
Life in Pictures. 7 April 2006 <http://
www.abamedia.com/rao/gallery/gagarin/>

The Age of the Female: A Thousand Years of Yin

Gandhi — Indian Child. <u>Mahatma Gandhi</u>. 9 April 2006
<http://www.indianchild.com/mahatma_gandhi.htm>

Graham — The Quotations Page. Martha Graham. 13 April 2006 <http://www.quotationspage.com/quote/1493.html>

Grolier — World War II Commemoration. 9 April 2006 <http://gi.grolier.com/wwii/wwii_mainpage.html>

H5N1 — CDC: Centers for Disease Control and Prevention. <u>Avian Influenza: Current Situation</u>. 10 April 2006 <http://www.cdc.gov/flu/avian/outbreaks/current.htm>

HIV — <u>The Origins of HIV and the First Cases of AIDS</u>. 10 April 2006 <http://www.avert.org/origins.htm>

Indian Independence — <u>Indian Independence Day Celebrations</u>. 9 April 2006 <http://www.123independenceday.com/indian/independence/day/>

Iowa — <u>Gender Equity in Sports</u>. U of Iowa. 9 April 2006 <http://bailiwick.lib.uiowa.edu/ge/>

Jefferson — BrainyQuote.com. Thomas Jefferson. 13 April 2006 <http://www.brainyquote.com/quotes/authors/t/thomas_jefferson.html>

JFK — The White House. <u>John Kennedy</u>. 9 April 2006 <http://www.whitehouse.gov/history/presidents/jk35.html>

JFK Assassination — Teaching Arts. <u>JFK Assassination and Funeral</u>. 9 April 2006 <http://teaching.arts.usyd.edu.au/history/hsty3080/StudentWebSites/AMELIA/My%20Webs/AMELIA%20RFK%20WEB/jfkassassfuneral.htm>

Johnson — Johnson, Steve Paul. <u>Doughboy Center:</u> The Great War Society. 9 April 2006 <http://www.worldwar1.com/dbc/arvetday.htm>

Jordan 1 — WomensHistory.com. Barbara Jordan Quotes. 13 April 2006 <http://womenshistory.about.com/od/quotes/a/barbara_jordan.htm>

Jordan 2 — QuoteLady.com. Barbara Jordan. 13 April 2006 <http://www.quotelady.com/subjects/responsibility.html>

Kilde — <u>Spekula: 3rd Quarter, October 23, 1999</u>. 12 April 2006 <http://www.raven1.net/kilde2.htm>

Kilde 2   Kilde, Rauni. Mind Controllers: Microchip
                   Implants, Mind Control & Cybernetics.
                   12 April 2006 <http://www.geocities.com/
                   hal9000report/hal36.html>

King   King, Richard. The King's Book of Numerology,
                   Vol.1:Foundations & Fundamentals. New
                   Brighton Books. Aptos. 2003.

King-Diana   King, Richard. Blueprint of a Princess: The
                   Numbers of Life and Death of Princess
                   Diana of Wales, manuscript. 1997

Langenkamp   SelfRealization.net. Langenkamp, Frans. The
                   Eternal Paradox of Free Will and
                   Predestination. 16 April 2006<http://
                   www.selfrealisation.net/VedicAstrology/
                   frwlbklt.htm>

MacArthur   Brainyquote.com Douglas MacArthur. 12 April
                   2006 <http://www.brainyquote.com/quotes/
                   authors/d/douglas_macarthur.html>

Microchip   Luukanen-Kilde, Rauni-Leena. Microchip
                   Implants, Mind Control, and Cybernetics.
                   Naturo-Doc. 12 April 2006 <http://
                   www.naturodoc.com/library/public_health/
                   microchip_implants.htm>

Mother Teresa   The Nobel Peace Prize, 1979 10 April 2006
                   <http://www.nobel.se/peace/laureates/
                   1979/presentation-speech.html>

Mukherjee   Mukherjee, Bharati. Time. Heroes and Icons.
                   10 April 2006 <http://www.time.com/time/
                   time100/heroes/profile/teresa02.html>

NASM, figure 1   Smithsonian National Air and Space Museum.
                   SI#: 97-15884-11. 7 April 2006 <http://
                   www.nasm.si.edu/galleries/gal114/>

National Archives, U.S. National Archives and Records
19th Amendment   Administration. 6 April 2006 <http://
                   www.archives.gov/exhibits/
                   featured_documents/amendment_19/
                   index.html>

Neil   Neil, Andrew. Interview with Jane Pauley. NBC

New York Academy   New York Academy of Sciences. Science and
of Sciences   the City. 11 March 2006 <http://
                   www.nyas.org/snc/
                   readersReport.asp?articleID=32<http://
                   www.quoteworld.org/quotes/4072>

Nobel Prize, King NobelPrize.org. Martin Luther King Biography.
                   9 April 2006 <http://www.nobel.se/peace/
                   laureates/1964/king-bio.html>

O'Connor and   O'Connor, J.J., and E.F. Robertson.
Robertson   Pythagoras of Samos. January 1999.
                          School of Mathematics and Statistics,
                          University of St. Andrews, Scotland. 9
                          March 2006
                          <http://www-groups.dcs.st and.ac.uk/
                          ~history/Mathematicians/
                          Pythagoras.html>.
Orwell   Brainyquote.com. George Orwell. 12 April 2006
                          <http://www.brainyquote.com/quotes/
                          authors/g/george_orwell.html>
Paine   Quote DB. Thomas Paine. 13 April 2006
                          <http://www.quotedb.com/quotes/1220>
Parks   Parks, Rosa. The Time 100. 9 April 2006
                          <http://www.time.com/time/time100/
                          heroes/profile/parks01.html>
Pioneer 10   NASA. Pioneer. 7 April 2006 <http://
                          spaceprojects.arc.nasa.gov/
                          Space_Projects/pioneer/PNhome.html>
Pioneer Plaque   7 April 2006 <http://www-
                          pw.physics.uiowa.edu/pioneer/ other/
                          plaque.gif>
Puri   Puri, J.R. Guru Nanak: His Mystic Teachings
                          Punjab. RSSB. 1993
Ranfranz   Ranfranz, Patrick. Charles Lindbergh, An
                          American Aviator. 2006 <http://
                          www.charleslindbergh.com/history/
                          index.asp>
Reagan   Quoteland.com. "Freedom." Ronald Reagan.
                          13 April 2006 <http://www.quoteland.com>
Ride   Chew, Robin. Sally Kristen Ride: First
                          American Woman in Space 1996. Lucid
                          Interactive. 7 April 2006 <http://
                          www2.lucidcafe.com/lucidcafe/
                          library/96may/ride.html>
Robinson   White House Dream Team: Jackie Roosevelt
                          Robinson 9 April 2006.<http://
                          www.whitehouse.gov/kids/dreamteam/
                          jackierobinson.html>
Sacagawea   Fact Monster. The Sacagawea Golden Dollar
                          10 April 2006 <http://
                          www.factmonster.com/spot/
                          sacagawea1.html>
SARS   Times On Line. 2003. <http://
                          www.timesonline.co.uk/article/
                          0..3-631739.00.htm>
Schrepf   Norbert, Verlag. Toy Soldier Gallery. Sir
                          Winston Churchill. 1999-2001. 9 April
                          2006 <http://www.toy-soldiergallery.com/
                          Articles/Churchill/Churchill.html>

Schweitzer   The Albert Schweitzer Fellowship. Quotes. 16 April 2006 <http://www.schweitzerfellowship.org/features/about/quotes.aspx>

Seneca Falls Convention   Background and Details. 4 April 2006 <http://americanhistory.about.com/library/weekly/aa040101a.htm>

Shepard   Alan Bartlett Shepard, Jr. Project Mercury Astronaut 7 April 2006 <http://www.pambytes.com/mercury-redstone3/shepard.html>

Singh   Singh, Sawan. Philosophy of the Masters, Volume 1. Punjab, India. RSSB. 1996.

Singh 2   Singh, Sawan. With the Three Masters: Volume 1. Punjab, India. RSSB. 1967. 140

Sputnik   NASA. Sputnik and The Dawn of the Space Age 2003 <http://www.hq.nasa.gov/office/pao/History/sputnik/>

Steel   Steel, Fiona. The Littleton School Massacre. Crime Library. 10 April 2006 <http://www.crimelibrary.com/serial4/littleton/>

Stewart   Business 2.0, November 2002. How To Think With Your Gut 11 April 2006 <http://money.cnn.com/magazines/business2/>

Stokesey   11 Nov. 2002 <http://www.stokesey.demon.co.uk/wwii/ahitler.html>

Tanenbaum   Seven Stories Press. 11 April 2006 <http://www.sevenstories.com>

Television History   Television History - The First 75 Years. 6 April 2006 <http://www.tvhistory.tv/EarlyTVBaird.htm>

Tereshkova   Enchanted Learning. Valentina Vladimirovna Tereshkova: The First Woman in Space 7 April 2006 <http://www.enchantedlearning.com/explorers/page/t/tereshkova.shtml>

Title IX   Title IX: Twenty-Five Years of Progress 9 April 2006 <http://www.ed.gov/pubs/TitleIX/>

Tomlin   BrainyQuote.com. Lily Tomlin. 13 April 2006 <http://www.brainyquote.com/quotes/authors/l/lily_tomlin.html>

TV Westerns   Shadows of the Past. 11 April 2006 <http://www.sptddog.com/sotp/tvwesterns.html>

U.S. Census Bureau, World Population	U.S. Census Bureau, Population Division, International Programs Center. Revised, 26 Apr 2005. Historical Estimates of World Population. 6 April 2006 <http://www.census.gov/ipc/www/worldhis.html>
U.S. Census, Midyear Population	U.S. Census Bureau, International Data Base. 4-26-2005 Total Midyear Population for the World: 1950-2050. 6 April 2006 <http://www.census.gov/ipc/www/worldpop.html>
USSR	The Cold War Museum. Fall of the Soviet Union. 9 April 2006 <http://www.coldwar.org/articles/90s/>
Wikipedia, Baird	Baird, John Logie. Wikipedia. 6 April 2006 <http://en.wikipedia.org/wiki/John_Logie_Baird>
Wikipedia, Earhart	Earhart, Amelia. Wikipedia. 7 April 2006 <http://en.wikipedia.org/wiki/Amelia_Earhart>
Wikipedia, Lindbergh	Lindbergh, Charles. Wikipedia. 7 April 2006 <http://en.wikipedia.org/wiki/Charles_Lindbergh>
Wilson	Brainyquote.com. Woodrow Wilson. 12 April 2006 <http://www.brainyquote.com/quotes/quotes/w/woodrowwil122747.html>
WTC-911	Chemtrail Central 10 April 2006 <http://www.chemtrailcentral.com/ubb/Forum6/HTML/000439.html>
WTC-First Attack	Commemorate WTC. June 2003 <http://commemoratewtc.com/history/firstattack.php>

The Age of the Female: A Thousand Years of Yin

Richard Andrew King
~ Books ~
www.richardking.net

The King's Book of Numerology
Volume 1-Foundations & Fundamentals

The King's Book of Numerology, Volume 1-Foundations & Fundamentals provides complete descriptions of Basic Numbers, Double Numbers, Purifier Numbers, Master Numbers, the Letters in Simple and Specific form as well as the Basic Matrix, the numerological blueprint of our lives.

"*The King's Book of Numerology* series contains new information that informs and predicts more completely and accurately than any previously published numerological work. It brings back the empowered sciences of long ago, information long since lost upon this plane." ~ G. Shaver

The King's Book of Numerology II
Forecasting – Part 1

The King's Book of Numerology II: Forecasting – Part 1 is dedicated to opening the door to the divine blueprint of our lives. That plan, that divine blueprint of destiny, is exact, precise, unchangeable, unalterable and . . . knowable, at least in general terms. Once this awareness of a predetermined fate becomes established through application of numbers and their truths, our understanding and consciousness of life will, no doubt, change. We will begin to see ourselves as part of an immense spiritual super-structure far beyond our current ability to comprehend, understand or perceive. Life will take on new meaning and, perhaps, we will even begin to awaken to greater spiritual truths. Subjects covered: Life Cycle Patterns, The Pinnacle/Challenge Matrix, Epoch Timeline, Voids, Case Studies and much more.

The King's Book of Numerology 3
Master Numbers

The King's Book of Numerology 3 – Master Numbers delves deeply into the subject of master numbers – multiple digit numbers of the same cipher, focusing especially on binary master numbers: 11-22-33-44-55-66-77-88-99.

Master numbers are the nuclear component of the numeric spectrum and play powerful roles in the destinies of individuals. They cannot be ignored.

KBN3 reveals the process of discovering hidden master numbers in all facets of a King's Numerology[tm] chart, how voids effect the life and much more.

The King's Book of Numerology 4
Intermediate Principles

The King's Book of Numerology 4 – Intermediate Principles will expand your consciousness of the mysteries of life and destiny by taking you deeper into the secret world of numbers and their meaning.

Life is energy. People are energy. Numbers are arithmetic codes describing and defining the energies that comprise our lives and destinies. Like priceless treasures discovered during an archaeological dig, numbers and number patterns buried beneath the surface of single numbers contain a treasure trove of untold wealth and secret riches of knowledge and wisdom.

Intermediate Principles chapters include Common Names, Linkage, Stacking, Name Suffixes, Binary Capsets, Influence/Reality Set Formats, Dual Basic Matrix Components, Subcap Challenges, and much more.

The King's Book of Numerology 5
I/R Sets – Level 1

IR SETS are the crux, core and substance of numerology forecasting, **indispensable** to the King's Numerology[tm] system and to anyone choosing to know where they've been, where they are now and where they're headed. They are obligatory for any serious and professional numerologist.

The King's Book of Numerology 5: I/R Sets – Level 1 offers a general explanation of each of the 81 IR Sets in order to create a foundation on which to build a greater understanding of how life's events affect us. KBN5 is a starting point from which to grow greater knowledge of one's self and destiny.

IR SETS are a gift for those willing to receive them, study them and apply their vast level of knowledge to make our lives more understandable, manageable, easier, better, whole.

The King's Book of Numerology 6
Love Relationships

This is a "stand alone" book. Its knowledge is not dependent on prior KBN publications. KBN6 contains the book *Your Love Numbers* plus its own Case Studies section.

KBN6 guides you through this revolutionary method of understanding the Secrets of Love and Happiness via the mystical science of numbers. If you can add 1 + 1, you can quickly learn how to utilize and benefit from the great truths shared within this book.

The fundamental Secret of all great relationships, marriages and partnerships revolves around the quality and quantity of *Mutual Energetic Resonance* between the partners. This resonance (MER) is easily identified from the natal data of the individuals involved – their full birth names and birth dates. In fact, this birth data is where the mysteries of everything, including love relationships and destiny, all begins.

The Age of the Female: A Thousand Years of Yin

Blueprint of a Princess
Diana Frances Spencer - Queen of Hearts

The tragic death of Princess Diana of Wales - the most famous, the most photographed, the most written about woman of the modern world and possibly of all time - was one of the most shocking and saddening events of the late Twentieth Century. Not since the assassination of American President John Fitzgerald Kennedy in 1963, has such an event captured the attention of the world. On that ill-fated Sunday of 31 August 1997, and the following week until her funeral, there was much discussion and reflection of the Queen of Hearts, the People's Princess, England's Rose. But in all of the media news coverage, there was no discussion given to the cosmic aspects of her life and death.

Blueprint of a Princess is dedicated to addressing those issues through The King's Numerology^{tm}. Its purpose and hope is to offer some consolation and explanation as to that one question so poignantly written on a card of condolence left with the multitude of flowers before the gates of Buckingham Palace. . . "Why?"

99 Poems of the Spirit

99 Poems of the Spirit draws from the writings of Perfect Saints, Masters, Mystics and Sacred Scriptures. Designed to lift the consciousness, mind and heart, all of the poems are original works by Richard Andrew King. Their purpose is to help connect the reader with the mystic side of life in order to enhance the process of self-realization while advancing on the spiritual path and climbing the ladder leading to the ultimate attainment of God Realization. It is a treasure chest of poetic spiritual gems offered to excite, educate and stimulate the mind and soul in the glorious journey of spiritual ascent.

Messages from the Masters
Timeless Truths for Spiritual Seekers

In a time where there is more need for enlightenment than ever before, *Messages from the Masters: Timeless Truths for Spiritual Seekers* offers timeless truths for genuine seekers thirsty for spiritual nectar.

Messages from the Masters is a rich source of hundreds of quotes from a cavalcade of nine Perfect Saints throughout the last six hundred years: Guru Ravidas, Kabir, Guru Nanak, Tulsi Sahib, Swami Ji Maharaj, Baba Jaimal Singh, Sawan Singh, Jagat Singh and Charan Singh. The messages in this book focus on the importance of the Divine Diet, the priceless Human Form, Reincarnation, the World, the Negative Power and Soul Food.

Warning! *Messages from the Masters* is not for the faint of heart or the worldly-minded. Masters come into the world to sever our attachment to it, not make it a paradise. Although the epitome of love and wisdom, they shoot straight from the hip, pull no punches, favor no religion. Their universal message of soul liberation is reflected in the statement of Saint Maharaj Charan Singh: *Just live in the creation and get out of it!*

The Age of the Female
A Thousand Years of Yin

The Age of the Female: A Thousand Years of Yin highlights the profound and extraordinary ascent of the female in the modern world, placing her center stage in the global spotlight as presidents and leaders of nations, titans of industry, corporate executives, military generals, media magnets, doctors, lawyers and a whole host of other prestigious titles normally associated with the male. Why has her rise to prominence been so rapid, especially in consideration of historic time? Why also has there been an increased interest in other people's lives in our society, in competitive athletics, personal data collection and the exploration of space and other worlds? *The Age of the Female: A Thousand Years of Yin* answers these questions. It is an insightful and exciting read into these mysteries, offering compelling and irrefutable evidence through the ancient science and art of numerology that, indeed, the age of the female has arrived and the next thousand years belong, not to him, but to her.

The Age of the Female II
Heroines of the Shift

The Age of the Female II: Heroines of the Shift continues the remarkable journey of the female's ascent in the modern world of the 2nd Millennium. This installment is a general read in five chapters honoring the accomplishments of women in categories of female firsts, female Nobel laureates, female athletes, female icons and female quotations.

The achievements of the women featured in *The Age of the Female II: Heroines of the Shift* are deserving of respect and admiration. Their lives, challenges and successes are motivational catalysts for every individual to be the best he or she can be and to honor the very essence of what it is to be human. *The Age of the Female II: Heroines of the Shift* is intended to be an inspiring and educational read for everyone, not just women but men, too, offering knowledge and insight of the depth, power and daring-do of women as their Yin energy rises upon the global stage in this millennium which destiny has irrefutably marked as the Age of the Female.

Your Love Numbers
Discovering the Secrets of Your Life, Loves and Relationships

NOTE: KBN6 contains this book, *Your Love Numbers*, plus Case Studies.

Your Love Numbers reveals the secret formula defining all great relationships and how to assess the love potential of any relationship in a matter of minutes.

Your Love Numbers teaches you how to assess a relationship or potential relationship in minutes, saving you endless time, energy, effort and possible heartache in the end. By knowing ourselves and the people we love, our relationships will be potentially more rewarding, satisfying, productive, peaceful, lasting and loving . . . for everyone - our family, spouses, partners, children, friends.

The Age of the Female: A Thousand Years of Yin

The Galactic Transcripts

The Galactic Transcripts will take you on a journey that is as provocative as it is mysterious. Its thirty-seven transmissions are channeled from a non-earth, alien group who identify themselves as members of the Space Brotherhood.

The Galactic Transcripts offer us descriptions of other worlds, their inhabitants, morals, ethics, and histories. They even forewarn of the coming cleansing of earth and the cataclysms preceding it. Other messages shed light on the original colonization of earth, telepathic communication, the power of love, the program of the Radiant One, and much more.

Those who have read *The Galactic Transcripts* have found them to be life-altering, profound, inspirational, transformative. Will they have that effect on you? Open your mind and allow the transcripts to take you beyond the limitations of our world and into new, undiscovered worlds far beyond our galaxy.

RichardKing.net
TheGalacticTranscripts.com

The Black Belt Book of Life
Secrets of a Martial Arts Master

The mystery and mystique of the martial arts is not only ages old, it's legend. Revered throughout the world, martial arts is a treasure chest of life secrets that transcend the boundaries of combat to include the expanse of life and living. Arguably, it is the greatest developmental system on earth for teaching the integration of body, mind and spirit

The Black Belt Book of Life: Secrets of a Martial Arts Master is not about physical fighting strategies and tactics. It is about concepts and principles we learn though martial arts training that can help us in the struggle of life, in the journey to conquer ourselves and gain the golden ring of our own completeness because in the end a true Black Belt should be a realized soul who, having engaged the enemy - himself - finds himself at the end of the journey, triumphant.

The Black Belt Book of Life: Secrets of a Martial Arts Master reveals many secrets of martial arts training, sharing these truths in quick and easy to read vignettes to benefit martial artists and the general public as well. It is a book for all readers, not just martial artists, both males and females, especially the youth of today who are in search of a foundation to guide their lives.

Destinies of the Rich & Famous
The Secret Numbers of Extraordinary Lives

Why are rich and famous people rich and famous? Is it luck? Hard work? Advantage by family name? What makes them special? What secrets are the basis of their success?

Destinies of the Rich & Famous explores the secret numbers of the following famous global icons and explains through The King's Numerology[tm] why they are both rich and famous - Dr. Albert Einstein, Amelia Earhart, Elvis Presley, General George Patton, Howard Hughes, John F. Kennedy, Marilyn Monroe, Michael Jackson, Muhammad Ali, Oprah Winfrey, Princess Diana and Sarah Palin

Destinies of the Rich & Famous answers these questions and much more. Too, it reveals the clear correlation between a person's life and his or her natal data - the date of birth and full name of birth, illustrating the reality that fame and fortune and destined!

DestiniesOfTheRichAndFamous.com

Parenting Wisdom
Raising Your Children By Their Numbers
To Achieve Their Highest Potential

This book is a must for any parent and all parents to be. It is vital to read this book now before you name your children. If you already have children, then it is just as important to understand them.

Richard Andrew King should be called Dr. King. His books are of the magnitude that will be read with reverence for generations to come. ~ Dr. Victoria Ford, J.D.

Parenting Wisdom for the 21st Century - Raising Your Children by Their Numbers to Achieve Their Highest Potential is a revolutionary addition to the process of arguably the most important job in the world, parenting.

The powerful information contained within this work will reveal the hidden desires driving your children, the paths they will follow in life, the roles they will give on the great life stage and much more – all designed to augment your parenting wisdom and support life's paramount parental purpose . . . to love the children and help them achieve their highest potential.

ParentingWisdom.net

Parenting Wisdom 2
What To Teach The Children

This work is a companion book to *Parenting Wisdom For The 21st Century – Raising Your Children By Their Numbers To Achieve Their Highest Potential.*

Parenting is the most important and critical job in life because it encompasses the cultivating and sculpting of life itself as reflected in our children – the sanctity of life in manifest form.

In the process of parenting one of the most germane questions is, "What do we teach the children?" Parenting Wisdom offers thirty-three time-tested, universal principles which parents can use to create a strong foundation allowing children to develop into whole, fulfilled, and substantive adults.

The thirty-three principles include: The Five Needs of Children, Boundaries, Rules, And Regs, Your Life, Your Responsibility, Tender Love Versus Tough Love, The Four Cornerstones of a Substantive Life, The Temptations of S.A.D. (Sex, Alcohol, Drugs) and much more . . .

ParentingWisdom.net

King

Richard Andrew King
~ CDs ~

RichardKing.net, CDBaby.com, and Online Retailers

Priceless Poetry & Prose 1
Dramatizations of Famous Literary Works

Wonderfully entertaining and educational artistic dramatizations of famous literary works for adults, children, teachers and students alike. Enjoy the timeless words of Shakespeare, Lincoln, Tennyson, Longfellow, Patrick Henry, Emily Dickinson, Chaucer and more.

Priceless Poetry & Prose 2
Selected Works of Edgar Allan Poe

Be enveloped in the mysterious and haunted world of one of America's most loved poets, Edgar Allan Poe. Highly entertaining and educational, enjoy classic poems such as, The Raven, Annabel Lee, Ulalume, Alone, Lenore and more.

Poems of the Spirit
Selected Original Poems of Richard Andrew King

A collection of original spiritual poems designed to edify the mind and uplift the spirit. Not for the faint of heart or worldly-minded, these works reflect timeless truths from scriptures, saints and mystics throughout the ages - messages enabling the individual to break the shackles of worldly ties in quest for spiritual realization.

Echoes from the Heart
Selected Original Songs of Richard Andrew King

An original collection of twelve of Richard's tug-at-your-heart ballads, cowboy songs, patriotic tributes and spiritual tunes for your soul. A few titles are *Waiting for You*, *Don't Forget the Heroes*, *One More Broken Heart*, *The Promise*, *Rodeo Cowboy*, *You Can't Push the River*, *No Itty Bitty Cowboy* and *Catch Me When I Fall*.

The Age of the Female: A Thousand Years of Yin

To order books, go to

www.RichardKing.net

Contact

Richard Andrew King

PO Box 3621

Laguna Hills, CA 92654

www.RichardKing.Net

The Age of the Female: A Thousand Years of Yin